Praise for Lou Holtz's

WINNING EVERY DAY
The Game Plan for Success

"Coach Holtz has written an inspiring and charming book in which he shares with us the gems of his experience as a great leader, devoted husband, and compassionate humanitarian. A quick and delightful read."

— GENERAL COLIN L. POWELL, USA (ret.)

"Seldom do we experience the charisma and character of a dynamic personality such as Lou Holtz, the very successful former football coach of Notre Dame. Lou has left his distinctive mark of success everywhere he has coached. 'Winning Every Day' is not just a catchy phrase, but with Coach Holtz, a way of life."

— CARL POHLAD, president,
Marquette Bancshare,
and owner of the Minnesota Twins

"*Winning Every Day: The Game Plan for Success* is a book for every would-be winner, whatever their occupation or goal in life might be. It is direct, clear-cut, concise, profound, humorous, wise, and precise in its recommendations for how to win every day, which will make a person a winner for life. Fun and easy to read, it's good, very good."

— ZIG ZIGLAR, author and motivational teacher

"Coach Holtz has a vast reservoir of knowledge and experience in the key elements of living a successful life. Using football as his primary vehicle, he provides a most inspiring and motivational treatise conveyed in a folksy and oftentimes humorous manner. Not only is *Winning Every Day* a very important book to read, but also a complete and utter joy."

—JOHN W. ("JAY") JORDAN, II, chairman and chief executive officer, Jordan Industries, Inc.

"Lou Holtz is a brilliant strategist, a first-class motivator, and an inspiring role model. *Winning Every Day* coaches you through the hard-won lessons of life that Coach Holtz has gleaned from a lifetime of learning. Using personal behind-the-scenes experiences, he shows you how to break through obstacles, capitalize on fleeting opportunities, and achieve success. There is no better mentor than Lou Holtz."

—PETER LOWE, president and chief executive officer, Peter Lowe International

"Lou has taken his wisdom and principles of winning on the gridiron and translated them successfully for implementation into daily life. He has also included his patented brand of humor throughout making this an informative as well as enjoyable read." —BARRY ALVAREZ, head football coach, University of Wisconsin

"Coach Lou Holtz has written one of the best motivational books that I've ever read on how to be successful in whatever you do in life." —STEVE SPURRIER, football coach, University of Florida

"Lou Holtz has spent most of his adult life helping others achieve their full potential. He believes success depends not so much on an abundance of God-given talent as it does on the passionate and intelligent application of the talent we have. *Winning Every Day* is the best of Lou Holtz."

—RICHARD A. ROSENTHAL, athletic director emeritus, University of Notre Dame

"The lessons contained in this book may start out having to do with sports, but they apply to almost every aspect of life. The stories in this book are wonderfully entertaining, and the lessons are priceless. This is a book about winning, written by a man who is a true winner in every sense of the word."

—SEAN MCMANUS, president, CBS Sports

"*Winning Every Day* provides a simple formula for a winning lifetime."   —DONALD R. KEOUGH, chairman of the board, Allen & Company, Inc.

"*Winning Every Day* is a great book for anyone who'd like to know Coach Holtz. His conversational writing style provides personal insight into a man whose ability to inspire and motivate is legendary. Lou Holtz's philosophy is easily adaptable and teaches you how to reach and exceed your goals, not only in athletics, but in business and daily living."

—CHRISTOPHER ZORICH, former NFL Chicago Bear, chairman, The Christopher Zorich Foundation

"I've known Lou Holtz for a long time as a man of unflinching, unyielding character and integrity. It shows in this remarkable book."   —SENATOR JESSE HELMS

"Lou Holtz has put into his book every element required for success in any endeavor. All who put into practice his ten elements for success will raise their level of performance significantly." —J. M. HAGGAR, JR., retired chairman of the board, Haggar Clothing Company

"This is the book we've all hoped Lou Holtz would write. In these pages he shares the wisdom and experience of a lifetime. It's a great read, and sure to be a hit."   —DAN QUAYLE, 44th vice president of the United States

"Lou Holtz is the best coach I have ever known. He is successful simply because of the standards and expectations he has of himself and those around him, and these are never compromised. In this book, Lou Holtz, the coach, the motivator, and the disciplinarian, gives you a plan for achieving a high standard of excellence in your life, family, or business. I had the privilege of working for Lou Holtz and learning the 'game plan' firsthand. He made a difference in my life, and he can make a difference in yours."
　　　　　　　　　　　　　　　　　　　—RICK MINTER,
head football coach,
University of Cincinnati

WINNING EVERY DAY

WINNING EVERY DAY

THE GAME PLAN FOR SUCCESS

LOU HOLTZ

FOREWORD BY
Harvey Mackay

A HarperBusiness book
from HarperPerennial

This book is dedicated to the women in my life: my precious daughters Luanne and Liz; my wonderful and special mother, Anne; my delightful mother-in-law, Eleanor; the finest person I have ever known, my wife, Beth, whom I love dearly; and last, but not least, our Blessed Lady on the Dome.

A hardcover edition of this book was published in 1998 by HarperBusiness, a division of HarperCollins Publishers.

HarperCollins books may be purchased for educational, business, or sales promotional use. For information please write: Special Markets Department, HarperCollins Publishers, Inc., 10 East 53rd Street, New York, NY 10022.

First HarperPerennial edition published 1999.

Designed by Joseph Rutt

The Library of Congress has catalogued the hardcover edition as follows:
Holtz, Lou.
    Winning every day : the game plan for success / Lou Holtz ; foreword by Harvey Mackay.—1st ed.
        208 p. ; 25cm.
    ISBN 0-88730953-4
    1. Holtz, Lou. 2. Success. 3. Conduct of life.
 GV 939.H59H65 1998
    98-199164

99 00 01 02 03 ❖/RRD 10 9 8 7 6 5 4 3 2 1

Contents

FOREWORD

Harvey Mackay

In the course of a lifetime, I've been in a lot of locker rooms. I've hooted and shouted with the winners. I've wept with the losers. But this was like no locker room I'd been in before.

There were about 100 bodies stuffed into the cramped, tucked-away locker room past the end zone in Sun Devil Stadium in Tempe, Arizona. Shoehorned into a corner of the coaches' dressing room along with a few other well-wishers, I took it all in. This was not your usual back-slapping, towel-snapping winners' ritual of self-congratulation. The players seemed frozen in front of their lockers. Joy was written on their faces, but they were subdued, expectant. We waited, all eyes turned in the same direction, the room falling silent as the words began.

"We didn't go out and try to win a national championship," said Coach Holtz. "We went out and tried to be the best we could be. And because you asked that of yourselves today and every day you choose to do that after today—for the rest of your lives—know this about yourself: You are a champion. You have it in you to always be a champion."

For these young men, this would be a—maybe the—highlight of their lives, a moment they would always cherish, whether or not they went on to glorious professional careers, football or otherwise.

What made the experience even more special was that it was uncompromised and untainted. Every opponent was legitimate, every victory genuine, every foot of ground and every touchdown earned. Notre Dame had finished the 1988 season as national champions with a perfect 12–0 record, beating Miami, then ranked number one; USC, then ranked number two; and finally, West Virginia, then ranked number three.

"You plan. You commit to excellence. And if it happens, if you achieve your highest goal, you have the reward of knowing it was by your efforts that you earned it. Today, that has happened. If someday it doesn't, if you don't always achieve your goal, be sure that it is not for want of trying. If you gave it the best you had in you, you cannot ask yourself for more. No one can ask you for more."

I've had the privilege of spending a good deal of time around Lou Holtz. What I've taken away from that relationship is not just a football experience. It's a life experience.

Being successful the Holtz way means more than being successful any way you can. Being successful the Holtz way means doing things the right way, the decent way. It is the way Lou Holtz coaches football, and the way he leads his life. Win or lose, the language and behavior in a Holtz locker room and on a Holtz team is at a different level than other locker rooms and other teams.

Lou Holtz is a 5'10", 150-pound giant.

When you'd see him on television, pacing up and down the sidelines, he seemed shorter and even more frail, in part because of the contrast between him and the behemoths standing around him, and in part because of the huge, thick glasses and clothes that always seem a size too big for him.

Up close, he seems bigger. If he's speaking to you one on one, even though he has a kind of lisp, he grows a bit more. In front of a group, as he was that day, he's not just an individual, he becomes so large he creates his own space, he's a presence.

I've seen him address groups of thousands, and I believe he's the best motivational speaker in the world.

Holtz once wrote a list of 107 personal goals. You'll read about them here. I know something about those 107 goals, and I suspect Holtz knows that same something, too. Just as soon as he finishes that list—and he *will* finish it—he's going to be miserable. Nothing to do. Nothing to love. Nothing to hope for. He's going to crumple his list into a little ball, throw it away, and make himself a new list.

Now, I've written enough nice things about Holtz. Being an age without heroes, it's time for the rough stuff.

Holtz is such a determined competitor, he will go to any legitimate length to gain an edge on an opponent.

This clouds his judgment.

Holtz will listen to anyone on the face of the earth who will give him a tip on how to improve his swing. Recently, we were in a cab in Phoenix, and the driver was telling us how he got a hot tip on the golf channel on television and cut a couple of strokes off his game. Immediately, Holtz made the driver stop the cab and demonstrate on the sidewalk of the corner of Scottsdale and Camelback exactly what he had learned.

No matter what Holtz writes here, I advise you not to take any golf advice from him. However, if my son or daughters were to ask me to name one person to go to outside of their old man for any other kind of advice, I'd name Lou Holtz.

INTRODUCTION:

THE GAME PLAN FOR SUCCESS

Winning is never accidental. All successful coaches and players—and I've known quite a few—have at least one thing in common: a strong game plan. I have seen teams short on talent win famous victories simply because they were better prepared, more focused than their opposition. They had clearly defined goals and consistent work habits. And they weren't afraid to make the sacrifices required to raise their play to another level.

If you want to achieve greatness in anything, you need the same resolve and discipline. You must design a strategy that will take you wherever you want to go. My hope is that this book will become your game plan for success. I have no literary pretentions; this isn't Faulkner or Le Carré resting in your hands. It never even occurred to me to write a book. But many people who have heard me speak have asked that I commit my game plan for success to paper. Once I agreed, my goal was to write a guide that was practical, easy to follow, and heartfelt. If reading my prose makes you feel as if you and I were chatting in your living room, that's exactly what I was aiming for.

Much of what I have to say is steeped in verities that may seem unfashionable in a world that often appears to be as cynical as it's sophisticated. But I believe they are powerful and enduring, of greater value today than ever before.

Right about now, you may be asking who does this Holtz guy think he is? What qualifies him to tell me what I need to do to win every day? Well, I'm with you. There's nothing extraordinary about me. However, I have done a few things that I am proud of:

I have been married to the same woman for 38 years. In a time when more than half of all marriages end in divorce, tell me that isn't a feat. All four of our children are college grads and, yes, they still speak to us. For two years running, an industry poll has selected me the best motivational speaker in the country. My tape, *Do Right!,* is the top selling motivational video of all time. I have appeared as a guest speaker before nearly every company listed in the Fortune 500.

Ever hear of the Lou Holtz Museum? I didn't think so. They have one in my hometown, East Liverpool, Ohio, and, all right, it's not as large as the Smithsonian, but even I was impressed when others had conceived of the idea. There is also a highway named after me, but on days when traffic is backed up that can be a dubious honor. Four different presidents have invited me to the Oval Office. Though I've retired from football, I still work as a TV analyst for CBS Sports. And, as of this writing, I am one of the top fifteen winningest coaches in college football history.

So much for the advertisements for myself.

I'm uncomfortable giving you my résumé. I always believed that when you achieve something you should let others talk about it rather than yourself. It's just my way of saying, "Look, with the help of many people, I've been able to accomplish some notable things. If I could do them, so can you because I am no more gifted than anyone who ever drew a breath."

It certainly wasn't superior intelligence that got me where I am. I graduated in the lower half of my high school class. At best, my I.Q. is average. I'm a TV commentator, so I must be a mesmerizing orator, right? As a matter of fact, I've had a pronounced lisp since childhood. It was so bad that when I was growing up in Follansbee, West Virginia, our family doctor wanted to operate on my tongue. They finally decided I would have to live with it. Which is exactly what I didn't do; I worked diligently to overcome this affliction until it was no longer an obstacle.

Since I have a football background, you might assume I was a standout athlete, a monster of the gridiron. Nope. I lived on the third team most of my life. I'm sure I could have been better if someone hadn't left my name off the guest list the day God handed out physiques. I'm 5'10", 150 pounds, wear thick glasses, and have the imposing, muscular body of a malnutrition poster boy. My family was poor. I was born in 1937—you've heard of the Great Depression—in a basement we rented. My father, a bus driver, never got past the third grade. No one from either side of my family had ever attended college.

Given my background, I know I have been blessed. Many people helped me get to where I am today, but much of what I've accomplished came out of a strategy I devised long ago. This book gives me the opportunity to share my good fortune. As you read it, you will quickly discover that choices are our game plan's bricks and mortar. Everything that happens to us is the result of the choices we make. You choose to act or procrastinate, believe or doubt, help or hinder, succeed or fail. My book is designed to help you put your game face on, to ensure that you are in a winning frame of mind every time you charge out onto the field.

The plan is composed of ten steps, each of them with their own importance. They've worked for me in my life and career. I'd like to think they've helped the colleagues, players, and business people I talk to so frequently:

1. **The Power of Attitude.** The attitude you choose to assume toward life and everything it brings you will determine whether you realize your aspirations. What you are capable of achieving is determined by your talent and ability. What you attempt to do is determined by your motivation. How well you do something is determined by your attitude.

2. **Tackle Adversity.** You are going to be knocked down. I have been on top and I have been at the bottom. To achieve success, you are going to have to solve problems. If you react positively to them, you'll be stronger and better than ever. You can assume that your competitors have problems, too. If you react to setbacks more quickly and positively, you gain a distinct advantage. I've never encountered a person who achieved anything that didn't require overcoming obstacles. Expect them.

3. **Have a Sense of Purpose.** Understand what you are trying to do. Stay completely focused on your original and primary purpose. Do not be sidetracked. If you own a business, help customers get what they want. If you want a promotion, give your employers what they want, somebody who delivers a first-rate performance every day.

4. **Make Sacrifice Your Ally.** You can't be successful without making sacrifices. Most losing organizations are overpopulated with people who constantly complain about life's difficulties. They will drain your enthusiasm

and energy. Take pride in making sacrifices and having self-discipline.

5.   **Adapt or Die.** Things are always changing, so embrace the fact that your life and career are always in transition. Yes, you will achieve your goals, but don't fall into the mistake of thinking you don't have to do anything further. Even when you become number one, you will still need to stay focused on the fundamentals.

6.   **Chase Your Dreams.** All great accomplishments start with a dream. Dreams fuel your enthusiam and vision. They give you a burning desire to get up in the morning and achieve.

7.   **Nurture Your Self-Image.** A positive self-image grows out of having strong character. To be trustworthy, committed to excellence, and show care for others are the underpinnings of a successful person. These qualities are so important I devoted the last three steps to each of them.

8.   **Foster Trust.** All relationships are based on trust. I can't begin to tell you how many people I have seen ruin tremendous opportunities because they didn't have the discipline and decency to do what's right. Continually ask yourself, "Is this the right thing to do?" Do what you feel is right regardless of peer pressure or personal desires; success and confidence will not be far behind.

9.   **Commit to Excellence.** Do everything to the best of your ability. Everybody wants to be associated with people who set and maintain high standards. When you lower standards, you only invite mediocrity.

10. **Handle with Care.** Treat others as you would like to be treated—with concern and care.

So that's the plan. It has been the blueprint for my success and I assure you that if you follow it, you will achieve all the things you have set out to do. But it's up to you. The only person that can change you is yourself. Not me, your boss, the president, or the pope. You.

Now let's suit up. And let's murmur a prayer for any opponents that dare get in our way. They're going to need all the help they can get.

1

EVERY VICTORY IS WON BEFORE THE GAME IS PLAYED: THE POWER OF ATTITUDE

I left the collegiate ranks in 1976 to sign a five-year contract to coach the New York Jets of the National Football League. This was one of the two or three most coveted coaching positions in pro football, with an organization known for its professionalism. Owner Leon Hess, an NFL pioneer, was a great leader who gave his employees maximum support. New York's football fans were knowledgeable and second to none in their enthusiasm. It was an ideal situation for any coach. Yet I was unhappy almost from the moment I took the job. Every time a problem surfaced—and no pro football team can go through an entire season without its share of travails—I immediately thought, "This isn't working out." When the Jets went an abysmal 3–10 during my first season, I resigned—only eight months into my contract.

Now let's look at the flip side of that experience. In 1983, the University of Minnesota hired me to coach its football team. Five coaches—and three assistant coaches—had refused this position. The reason? Minnesota's football program had been in shambles for some time. The team, known as the Gophers, had just compiled an ignominious 17-game losing streak in which they were outscored by an average of 34 points per game. No one believed the school could quickly reverse its fortunes.

I declined the job when Minnesota's administration initially offered it to me. Besides having the same doubts as my colleagues, I couldn't see myself living in the tundra that was Minnesota. Harvey Mackay—the world-famed entrepreneur and best-selling author of *How to Swim with the Sharks Without Being Eaten Alive*—had to use all his considerable persuasive powers to convince me to accept the position. Am I glad he did. Minnesota proved to be a great place to live. The people were friendly, the fans exuberant, and the climate not quite arctic.

I made up my mind early on that we were going to create a winning atmosphere. Fan morale was low when I took over the team. Attendance had declined for years; Minnesota often played its games before a half-filled house. However, only one year after I joined the Gophers, we sold 54,000 more season tickets—11,000 more than had been sold at any time during the school's 103-year history. Our winning record earned us an invitation to play Clemson in the Independence Bowl. You couldn't have asked for a more rousing success.

What made the difference between my experiences with the Jets and Gophers? Attitude. I joined the Jets suspecting I might fail; I came to Minnesota determined to win. With this positive outlook, I wasn't flustered when obstacles appeared. I knew we would overcome them. All that had changed was my perspective and, with that, my results. If I ever coach pro ball again, I promise you I'm going to bring that same "can-do" attitude with me.

Your talent determines what you can do. Your motivation determines how much you are willing to do. Your attitude determines how well you do it. For example, imagine you're a high jumper with the musculature to leap 6'10". Your pride of performance motivates you to practice and enter events. But if, on the day of the event, you don't believe you can hit 6'10", you're going to fall short of the mark. Your negative attitude will cut inches from your performance. However, compete with a certitude that you will clear 6'10" and you will consistently match or better your expectations. A positive attitude is the key to attaining superior altitude.

Sweeter Than Any Bowl of Cereal

No one can control your attitude but you. Yet too often we let other people or external circumstances determine how we feel. In 1991, our team, the Fighting Irish of Notre Dame, was selected to play the University of Florida in the Sugar Bowl. Florida's Gators were formidable opponents. Their coach, Steve Spurrier, was (and is) a brilliant leader and tactician. Gator quarterback Shane Matthews was a superior talent blessed with a strong arm and a field commander's presence.

No one thought we could win this game. In fact, we were such a decided underdog that many people wondered if we could even hold the score close. But I believed we were poised to upset the Gators. Our team couldn't have been better prepared, and I knew our players were brimming with confidence.

A few days before the Bowl, I took my family to dinner in Orlando. We were talking about the upcoming game and my family could see how optimistic I was about our chances. I felt like I was on top of the world. While taking our order, the waiter scrutinized me a bit before asking, "Aren't you Lou Holtz, the Notre Dame coach?" When I told him I was, he said, "Let me ask you a question. What's the difference between Notre Dame and Cheerios?" I didn't know. He answered, "Cheerios belong in a bowl, Notre Dame doesn't." It was meant to be a joke, but I couldn't find any humor in it. You want to talk about a radical change in attitude! I am here to tell you I was upset.

However, I remained outwardly calm. I said to the waiter, "It's my turn to ask you a question. What's the difference between Lou Holtz and a golf pro?" He said, "I don't know." I replied, "Golf pros give tips, Lou Holtz won't." Now if I didn't believe with all my heart that we were going to win that game, I would have left that dining room in a permanent funk. Those pesky gremlins of self-doubt would have been working at my ear. I may have started to question our ability and, believe me, that would have adversely affected our performance.

Instead, I shrugged off my anger and reminded myself that I knew what our team could do; it didn't matter what anybody else thought. That's the attitude you have to carry into life. You can't let the naysayers pull you down. Remember: If someone says you can't accomplish something, it is an opinion and nothing more. It only becomes a fact when you tell yourself that you can't do a task. (By the way, we upset the Gators in that Sugar Bowl. When they blew the game's final whistle, sealing our victory, the first person I thought of was that waiter. I had the most satisfying image of him sitting at home, crying into his Cheerios.)

A Passion for Leadership

As a leader, your attitude has a powerful impact on others. Whether that impact is positive or negative depends on the choices you make. You have an obligation to develop a positive attitude, one that inspires the people around you to achieve the impossible. Great leaders also possess a passion for their causes. If enough people care, there isn't any problem in this world we can't solve. Sexism, racism, spousal abuse, poverty, all the great ills afflicting our society would evaporate. However, most of us are too unconcerned to act on our own; we need leaders to stoke our passions. If you want to lead, that is the responsibility you must accept. And it starts with your own fervor. You can't fake it. If you don't have a genuine hunger to accomplish something, you won't be able to lead anyone effectively. But if you have a passion, you'll find it's an infectious thing. You'll transmit it to others who will pledge heart and soul to your principle.

Cotton Bowl 1988: A Turning Point

In 1987, my second year at Notre Dame, our football team took an 8-1 record into our season's final two games. Unfortunately, the first of those contests came against a tough Penn State squad on one of the coldest days I have ever experienced as a coach. We lost 21–20 when our two-point conversion failed in the game's last minute. Talk about disappointing losses. We never fully recovered from it. One week later, we traveled down to play Miami, another powerful opponent, in our season finale. We didn't play well that day, so we finished our season at 8–3.

That was a respectable record—though not by Notre Dame standards. Under normal circumstances, we might not have played any more football that season. However, the Bowl bids that year had gone out earlier than usual. When we were still 8–1, we had been invited to play Texas A&M, coached by Jackie Sherrill, in the Cotton Bowl. I must tell you that the Bowl officials weren't too delighted when we dropped those last two games, but we thought we belonged there.

For the first portion of the Cotton Bowl, so did everyone else. Our defense played tough, and by second quarter's midpoint, we led Texas A&M 10–0. Unfortunately, we played poorly the rest of the afternoon; Sherrill's team beat us decisively. I couldn't have been more dejected when I walked into the locker room after that game. But most of our players appeared unfazed.

Only one of them seemed as distraught as I. Chris Zorich, a sub who hadn't even played that day, was crying deep, gut-heaving sobs. There was the passion I wanted to see! As I looked around the locker room, I decided that next year's team would be composed of players who loved this game as much as he did. Chris would be in our starting lineup for the 1988 season; we would see to it that he was joined by a band of fire-eaters, guys who believed in themselves and what we were trying to accomplish.

We were going to need them. Notre Dame was about to lose a group of talented seniors such as receiver Tim Brown, our Heisman Trophy winner. The next season didn't look too promising on paper, but fortunately paper doesn't count for much; you still have to play the games. And besides, I had an agenda that went beyond our on-field performance. Win or lose, I wanted to coach the team with the best attitude in the entire country.

There was one senior on our team by the name of Flash Gordon who wanted to return for his fifth year of ball. He had been a starting defensive end in '87, but due to an injury he had sustained earlier in his college career, he still had another year of eligibility remaining. Knowing the kind of players I was looking for, I advised Flash to forget football; I doubted he would start for us and felt he would regret any decision to return to our team.

I wanted a particular attitude to permeate our 1988 squad. What I envisioned was probably best summed up by a poster

I had seen that depicted a buzzard sitting on a tree limb while saying, "Patience, my ass. I'm going to kill somebody."

I expected everyone on our team to think that way; Flash had never demonstrated that kind of makeup. Now understand, Flash is one of the finest young gentleman I have ever known. He was hard-working, loyal, and popular with the other players and students. His attitude couldn't have been more positive. But he didn't have any predator in him; he wasn't like that big, bad buzzard on the poster.

When the two of us met to discuss his future, Flash did everything he could to persuade me to accept his return. I finally relented with this caveat: "If you present the first bit of a problem for us, I will not hesitate to suspend you." I actually had no real justification for taking such a harsh tone; Flash was a class act. However, I wanted him to understand how integral a proper attitude was to our future success.

Flash started the first couple of games on our 1988 schedule, but was soon replaced by freshman defensive end Arnold Alle. Gordon had played decently, but we wanted to give Arnold a chance to earn the starting position. During the middle of the season, we met the University of Pittsburgh on their home field; Flash barely played that day. It had to be a bitter afternoon for him; Pittsburgh was his hometown.

The following week we met the University of Miami, a classic confrontation between two outstanding teams. Flash Gordon again played a minimal role in the game and had few opportunities to make a substantial contribution. Throughout all this, Flash's attitude remained positive and team-oriented. However, on the Monday afternoon following the Miami contest, Flash revealed his unhappiness. He entered my office and said, "Coach, I don't think I'm being treated fairly." Flash pointed out that he had done everything he could possibly do to help the football team even though he hardly ever played. Now he was asking for a square deal. He said, "I don't believe I'm being appraised by the same standard as the other players at my position."

I allowed him to make his case, which he did eloquently. Then I replied, "Flash, I really appreciate the wonderful attitude you have displayed this entire season. Let me get the defensive coordinator and your position coach and we'll review your situation." I brought in both coaches. We studied his grades and production as compared to the other defensive ends. The facts were clear: Flash was right. He had performed as well if not better than anybody at his position. I said, "Flash, we will see that you get back on the field. How much you play after that will be entirely up to you."

You know what? Over the final five games of the season, Flash Gordon wasn't good, he was phenomenal. When we played for the National Championship, he turned his game up several notches; he may have been our most outstanding defensive player. I am not sure we could have won that championship without Flash's on-field contribution, but it was his attitude off the field that was even more important to our success. And, of course, we couldn't have won without Chris Zorich, the young man whose cloudburst after the Cotton Bowl helped convince me we needed to alter the chemistry on our team. Chris went from sub to starter to team captain. He was one of our primary leaders when we won the National Championship, which was fitting, since he helped start our turnaround.

Talking Ain't Doing

I don't believe you can change anybody's attitude with even the most inspiring pep talk unless it is supported by results. I remember when I was in high school my coach gave us the greatest pep talk I have ever heard; Knute Rockne would have envied him. I don't think I have ever been as fired up for a football game as I was that night. I ran down under the opening kickoff filled with spit and fire. Then some guy hit me in the jugular vein with his helmet, knocking me flat. Suddenly, I couldn't remember a word the coach had said. I just lay there making little whimpering sounds. As my teammates helped me up, I left my positive attitude lying somewhere on that field.

An Unstoppable Force

I love to tell the story about the army private who had pulled KP duty. After twelve hours of peeling potatoes, he came back to the barracks exhausted. He was so bone-tired he could barely manage to drop his worn body on the bed. Didn't even bother to take off his clothes. As he rolled over to catch some much needed Z's, he noticed there was a letter from his girl on his pillow. He quickly opened it and read, "Dear John: If I could feel your strong masculine arms embrace me one more time, if I could gaze into those big crystal blue eyes of yours one more time, or if I could taste your sweet, tender lips just one more time, I know I could continue to be true, but . . ." John didn't bother to read anymore. He jumped from the bed and took off. Forget how fatigued he was, this was a man on a mission.

John was running off the military post—doing the 100 in about 9.5—when he approached the guardhouse. The guard on duty saw him coming, took out his M–14 rifle, and aimed it at John's heart. "Halt or I'll shoot," he shouted. John never broke stride. He left the guard no option. The very last words John uttered were these: "My mother is in heaven, my father is in hell, my girl is in Chicago, and I'm going to see one of them tonight." That's what I call a determined attitude. This boy could have played for one of my teams anytime.

People Can't Change, Huh? Ask Mr. Bettis

When Jerome Bettis left the University of Notre Dame to enter the NFL, he was a great football player, an unyielding competitor with a true warrior's attitude. No one who knew what he was made of was surprised when the media named him the NFL's Rookie of the Year. While playing for the Los Angeles Rams during that first season, he had been a human wrecking ball, the talk of the league.

Unfortunately, he regressed somewhat the following year; his decline continued throughout his third year. If you are going to understand Jerome, you have to know that most players would have been delighted with the stats Jerome compiled during those three years. But the numbers weren't up to his standards. He knew he was capable of doing more.

During our football season, I didn't have a chance to see a lot of pro games. However, an open date in November gave me an opportunity to catch a Rams contest. I was eager to watch Jerome and Notre Dame alum Todd Lyght, Los Angeles's gifted cornerback, compete. Jerome's performance disappointed me.

When you are a leader and you know someone is under-achieving, you must know how to push his or her buttons. I had an idea how to get through to Mr. Bettis. I phoned him the following day and said, "Jerome, I would like you to know that there is some idiot wearing a jersey with your name and number on it. This pretense is damaging your reputation. This guy is not picking up linebackers, is not running hard enough, and is not competing with enthusiasm, so I know it's not you, because you have never played like this before. I just thought I ought to let you know that this idiot is doing this. See if you can't put a stop to it, because he's giving you a bad name." Then I hung up.

On the first day of classes for the following semester—January 17 on my calendar—Jerome came to my office to say, "Coach, you were right. When I left here I had a great attitude and now I don't. I've returned to Notre Dame to get it back." And you know what? That's exactly what he did. When Bill Cowher of the Pittsburgh Steelers acquired him during the off-season, I knew Jerome was going to resurrect his career. Cowher was the perfect match for him. I had recruited and coached Bill at North Carolina State. Since then, he had become one of the NFL's best coaches; I knew he had a knack for developing a player's attitude. Jerome has thrived under him. He has made All-Pro for the past two years and is going to be a force in the NFL for many seasons to come. His career revival demonstrates how you can change your attitude for the better if you're willing to make the commitment.

A Missed Punt of My Own

Before every home football game at Notre Dame, we hold a sit-down luncheon in the Joyce Athletic Center. Nearly 3,000 people attend. This luncheon was always a sellout; the demand for tickets was so high, some folks sold them at scalper prices. The people who couldn't get in—about 1,000 to 1,500 of them—would commandeer seats in the hockey arena located at the end of the Center just so they could hear the program.

As part of our presentation, I would introduce three football players, who would stand before the audience and discuss their most memorable Notre Dame experiences. An assistant coach would follow with a short talk. Then I would rise to answer audience questions.

This was always an upbeat affair; the players usually thanked their parents and various other people before relating their stories. You couldn't help but be impressed by the eloquence of these fine young men. I cannot remember listening to a single athlete who didn't make me proud to be his coach. However, there was one speaker who genuinely shocked me: Craig Hentrich, probably the best punter in Notre Dame history. Craig rose after I had given him a lavish introduction. I expected Craig to follow tradition and regale us with warm stories about all the wonderful times he had enjoyed at South Bend.

Instead, he launched into a tirade about how unfairly I had treated him. Craig claimed that I lacked a genuine appreciation for his talents. As evidence of this, he pointed out that I was the only coach in America who traveled with one kicker and two priests. Every other school had two or three kickers on their teams, but, according to Craig, bringing an extra priest meant one less kicker. He went on to lament how he never had anybody to talk to during pre-game warm-ups.

Craig continued in this vein for what felt to me like a small eternity before finally sitting down. I got up, looked at him, and ad-libbed, "If you kicked a little better, we would only need one priest." The audience laughed uncontrollably but, believe me, I got Craig's message. I didn't agree with all of it. I *did* realize how important the kicking game was; we always worked hard on this singular phase of our game. If you check the stats, you'll discover that year in and year out, we had one of the best kicking games in the country. But I must admit that I could have been more demonstrative of my appreciation for his efforts.

Leaders must know what motivates their people. Some will not do their best until you kick them in the butt; others need continual pats on the back. Craig obviously needed some stroking. I should have gone out of my way to let him know how integral he was to Notre Dame's success. I respected his dedication and commitment to excellence. I should have told him that. Had I taken the time, Craig's attitude would have been better; he probably would have been even more productive than he was. Which would have been something to see, since Craig still holds most of Notre Dame's kicking records and was one of the fiercest competitors I have coached. He went on to punt for the Super Bowl Champion Green Bay Packers and just recently signed a $5 million dollar contract to play with the Oilers.

You Have to Identify the Problem Before You Can Solve It

I have also seen how events can adversely affect the attitude of an individual or a team and consequently hurt their performance. During my final year at Notre Dame, we started the season 3–0. After beating the University of Texas in Austin with an inspired effort, I came home eager to prepare the team for our next opponent—mighty Ohio State. The game was scheduled for our own turf, and I knew it was going to be a war.

There is no greater feeling for a coach than the one he gets when he walks onto the practice field the Monday before a big football game. Your adrenaline is racing. Team morale is soaring and the camaraderie between your players is palpable. Everyone is focused on the same goal. The energy is so high you would swear the playing field was radioactive.

At least, that's how it's supposed to be. So you can imagine how disappointed I was when I encountered an entire team of unmotivated players at our first practice. When they took the field it looked as if they were just going through the motions. We could have not been flatter. And it wasn't as if we were simply having a bad day. The team's nonchalance continued throughout the week. This concerned me. However, instead of doing something about it, I rationalized that the players were probably preoccupied with their academics. Looking back, though, that would not have explained why the team seemed so out-of-character. They weren't merely listless; they seemed divided. I started getting paranoid. I even entertained the notion that someone was deliberately sowing the seeds of disloyalty among us. I'd never seen anything like this.

Of course, it never occurred to me that the team might be suffering a collective crisis of confidence. We were the Fighting Irish of Notre Dame. Our script called for us to make the other team apprehensive, not the other way around. Whatever was dogging us, neither I nor the team could shake it. When we played Ohio State, we were as flat in the game as we had been all week during practice. They soundly whipped us in a game I thought we would win.

Oh, did that loss give my confidence a bruising. I returned home disappointed after that game—in myself, not the players. I wondered if the problem was me. Had I lost my ability to inspire our players? For the first time, I considered quitting. I later discovered that a variety of factors had contributed to our poor attitude and subsequent loss. It had nothing to do with my motivational skills. The root cause was an incident that occurred the night of our victory over Texas A&M. It would serve no useful purpose to recount what happened in detail; none of our players were directly involved in the incident, but it affected everyone on the squad. I didn't learn all of the facts until much later in the season.

I have to take some blame for that. When I saw our team's incohesiveness, I should have done everything I could to discover the cause. Rationalization and speculation did not get the job done. I should have called a team meeting, locked the doors, and announced that no one was leaving until we uncovered our problem. As a leader, you are responsible for everything that occurs on your watch. If you notice morale drooping, you must take decisive action before the situation becomes chronic and jeopardizes your entire organization.

Communication Erases Obfuscation

As you can see, leaders must be able to instinctively evaluate their organization's mind-set. Experience plays a big hand in this. When you work with someone for a year or more, you should know them well enough to understand what moves them. You will work with some people who aren't afraid to show their emotions. When they have problems, everyone knows it. They are easy to measure and anticipate.

More difficult to read are those people who shield their feelings. You'll need keen communication skills to reach them. You can read many books on the subject, but I think mastering communication is a cinch. All you have to do is remember that the Lord gave you two ears and one mouth because he wants you to listen twice as much as you speak. Communication also means availability. You can't be an absentee leader. If people see you often, they are more likely to feel comfortable in your presence and you'll have more opportunities to learn who they are through observation. Don't be aloof. I think every leader should mingle with his or her troops. You should also schedule regular, informal confabs where everyone can speak their minds freely, air gripes, and make useful suggestions. It's an excellent way to let everyone know your communication lines are open.

I maintained an open-door policy wherever I coached and so should you. My athletes, particularly the seniors, usually had no compunction about visiting me if they had a problem or disagreed with one of my decisions. (This is what made the Ohio State affair such a mystery. No one had offered me even a hint of what was behind it.) When people bring you a problem or gripe, show them respect and concern. Let them make their points while you listen dispassionately. Make no judgments until they are finished. Even if you eventually reject what they have to say, they should leave knowing they received a fair hearing. Otherwise, you'll discourage future communication. If you manage a large group, communicating with all of them regularly may be difficult. Appoint people you trust to act as liaisons. They should function like team captains who let the head coach know about problems before they become catastrophes.

I also kept communication lines open on our teams by appointing advisory committees. These were usually composed of eight to ten seniors, five or six juniors, and two or three sophomores, not necessarily starters, but people who cared deeply about our team. I knew each of them wouldn't hesitate to voice any disagreements they had with me.

When You're Loaded with Criticism, Don't Pull the Trigger

Never be overly critical of an individual's performance. First, find out why he or she failed. You might be unaware of some physical or emotional factors. I've seen athletes who looked as if they weren't hustling. It was only when I questioned their commitment that I discovered they were hiding an injury. They were actually too dedicated. You can awfully foolish when something like that happens.

When people on your team perform poorly, you must also make sure they understand their objectives. Have they been trained appropriately to meet these objectives? Do they understand their roles in your overall scheme? Are there any personal problems hampering their performances? Look at these elements before questioning their attitude or ability.

I Know We're the Fighting Irish, But . . .

In 1989, we were playing Southern Cal at home. Just as our pre-game warm-up ended, a fight erupted in the end zone between some SC and Notre Dame players. I was so upset in the locker room after the melee, I didn't care whether we won the game. What made this so frustrating was that I had warned our players before they took the field that something like this might happen. I had exhorted them to control their tempers. Under no circumstances were they to engage in a fight. The typical pre-game brawl usually involves athletes who know they won't see much playing time that day. They have all this energy built up and they have to release it. Sometimes all it takes is a dirty look, or what a player interprets to be a dirty look, and the nonsense begins. After the game, the perpetrators go back to the dorm, do a little male bonding, and congratulate themselves for kicking someone's tail.

That kind of thuggish behavior has no place in football. I let my team know how disappointed I was in their lack of restraint. My dressing down sapped much of the squad's spirit. I've rarely seen any team of mine play a worse two quarters. By the end of the first half, we were down 21–7. Southern Cal had a fine football team, but we were beating ourselves. As we hit the locker room, I knew it was time for an attitude adjustment.

I had made a mistake with my pre-game speech. At the time, my players were still seething over that end-zone altercation. They had wanted at SC in the worst way, and I had taken all the fight out of them. My browbeating had pushed the wrong buttons. Now I had to constructively re-stir their rage. I had plenty of ammunition. Though no longer upset over the fisticuffs, I was now thoroughly embarrassed by our inept play. I vented my feelings to the team during my half-time talk. When we took the field for the third quarter, our attitudes had done a 180. It was a completely different team that went on to win the game, 28–24. I doubt any Notre Dame team ever played a finer half of football during my tenure with the school.

Downsizing the Big Mo

People discuss momentum in sports all the time, but have you every heard anybody adequately define what it is? Momentum is nothing more than a state of mind. Again, an attitude. For example, you are winning a football game 14–0. Your opponent scores just before the half to make it 14–7. Up in the broadcast booth, the announcers proclaim that momentum has just swung in favor of the other team, even though you're still ahead 14–7. Now let's look at another game. This time your team is tied at 7–7. You score a touchdown and make the extra point just before the half to go ahead 14–7. As you enter the locker room, everyone now claims the momentum is with you. Ridiculous. The score is 14–7 in both instances. In other words, momentum is whatever your attitude determines it to be.

Dare to Make Your Own Miracles

In the early 1980s, I was coaching for the University of Arkansas. We were undefeated entering our sixth game of the season against Baylor. That was a fine football team with two outstanding running backs, Dennis Gentry and Walter Abercrombie, who both went on to play several years in the NFL. In addition, they had Mike Singletary, a middle linebacker who was awfully good.

We were a touchdown favorite to win that day, but Baylor beat us every which way but loose during the first half. With barely five minutes left in the third quarter, we were losing 17–0. I thought we were lucky to be that close. Our team hadn't smelled a first down all afternoon, let alone score a touchdown. Now we faced a fourth-and-six situation at mid-field. And the clock was ticking. It was obvious that we were going to lose the game unless we did something drastic. So we decided to pass instead of punt. Any chance we had of winning the game hinged on this play. If our quarterback failed to complete his pass, it would be time to call in the dogs.

On the sidelines, we decided against attempting anything for short yardage and the down. Hey, if you're sitting in a poker game without any pairs and the other guy is holding four aces, there is only one thing you can do—kick over the table! We chose to let it all hang out with a deep bomb to Bobby Duckworth, which he caught for a touchdown. Our team was finally on the scoreboard.

We needed that big play. When you bet the entire pot and win, you can jolt your entire organization from its malaise. As soon as Bobby scored, our fans and players got psyched. Yes, we were still down by 10, but we had given our attitudes a jolt with a daring call. Now everyone on the team believed we could pull this game out. Baylor's Grant Teaff, a splendid man and great football coach, could do absolutely nothing to stop us once we scored that touchdown. We dominated his team on offense and defense for the remainder of the game to win by ten points.

I would like to tell the reader that I have lost some games which we appeared to have won. Always remember, as long as your opponent has life, don't let that sucker up until he concedes.

Standards Don't Choose You

Never take your attitude for granted. Reevaluate yourself continually to ensure you are maintaining your edge. I remember when we moved Andy Heck, a fine starting tight end for Notre Dame, to offensive tackle. The switch required Andy to make a difficult adjustment. One spring afternoon after a scrimmage, I happened by our meeting room while the offensive linemen were viewing a film. I heard Andy complain to his offensive line coach, Joe Moore, that he had received a negative grade on a particular play which he thought he had performed adequately. Coach Moore shut off the film and said, "Andy, that would be true for an average player, but I don't think you are an average player. Do you want me to grade you as an average player so your mark will be positive? Or should I grade Andy as a great player, in which case your performance on that play was a minus. Which do you choose?"

Coach Moore didn't have to say another word. Andy chose to think of himself as a great player; he immediately elevated his personal standards. Andy went on to become team captain and has played with distinction for the past seven years in the NFL. He is presently with the Chicago Bears and one of the better offensive tackles in the entire league. Andy's obvious talent has played only a partial role in his accomplishments. I believe his career as a pro football star improved the day Coach Moore's questions forced him to make an attitude check.

I hope I've made myself clear how your attitude has the power to change your life. What should you do if you don't have a positive outlook? Find one. Instead of thinking "I can't," start saying "I can!" It takes just as much time and energy. If you are surrounded by a lot of negativists, think about putting some distance between yourself and them. Surround yourself with people who encourage rather than discourage. Read books or watch films depicting the lives of people who overcame great odds. If they could do it, so can you. Think about winning before you go to sleep and the moment you wake. Remember: Every day, some ordinary person does something extraordinary. Today, it's your turn.

2

THE BEST PART OF GETTING KNOCKED DOWN IS GETTING BACK UP: TACKLING ADVERSITY

I've told every team I ever coached that we would encounter at least three crises a season. Our success would depend on how we reacted to these threats. Every team and organization has its share of setbacks. It's not enough to overcome them. You must also learn from them. The great jazz musician Miles Davis once said, "Don't be afraid of failure. There is no such thing." I endorse that thinking. As you read this chapter, I think you'll see there isn't a single predicament you can't convert into a plus. You just have to remember: *Don't let what you don't have keep you from using what you do have.*

My Inspiration

This chapter on adversity is a difficult one for me. I am writing it while my wife Beth is undergoing cobalt treatments for throat cancer. A physician, using an incorrect procedure, misdiagnosed her biopsy last January. For six months, her undetected cancer spread throughout her entire throat. When they finally diagnosed her condition correctly, the doctors had to perform eleven and a half hours of surgery to excise the growth. As I write this, she has been undergoing three radiation treatments a day, five days a week, for nearly seven weeks. My family and I have never faced greater adversity than this dreadful disease. Through it all, my wife has been a champion. I have never seen anyone confront any hardship with so much grace and courage. And she, with her strong religious faith, has been a tremendous inspiration not only to me but to everybody who has seen how well she has handled this troublesome period.

My wife couldn't be more unlike me. If she feels down, she hides it. When I'm down, I not only let people know, I want them to be as miserable as I am. This is not one of my positive traits, and it is something I must work on.

We could complain about the terrible things that befall us, but that would be a waste of time. Adversity is a part of life. I have never met anyone who achieved success without first overcoming some misfortune. I'm sure if I asked you to discuss your accomplishments, you would highlight the obstacles you overcame to achieve your goals. Did you know that Thomas Edison went through 5,000 different elements before discovering the one that enabled him to invent the electric lightbulb? He could have stopped after his five hundredth miss and no one would have called him a quitter, but he kept working toward his goal while learning from every failed attempt. Like all winners, he saw his obstacles as opportunities.

You Aren't Good Enough to Get Mad!

I've always had to carry my share of adversity. When I coached the University of Arkansas, they made a state hero out of me after our victory against Oklahoma. They voted me into the local Hall of Fame, even issued a doll featuring my likeness. The following year, we lost a big game to Texas and sales of that doll tumbled. They couldn't give them away. I believe the only people who were buying them were using them as targets on their dartboards. Arkansas fans were so displeased, I thought they were going to burn me in effigy. So I know what it's like to fall from the heights in a hurry.

When I was coaching at North Carolina State, Johnny Durr—television's most popular golf commentator at the time—invited me to play Pinehurst #2 with his party. I did not swing my clubs particularly well that day. On the sixth hole, we came to a par 3. I asked Johnny what club I should use. I should have asked him the distance to the hole, but didn't think of it. Johnny recommended a six iron. After following his advice, I whacked the ball dead on the sweet spot. It was as good a six iron as I have ever hit. As it sailed toward the pin, I could see the headlines, "Lou Holtz Nails a Hole in One!" Unfortunately, my ball did not cooperate. Instead of dropping into the hole, it sailed over the pin, then rolled down a hill.

I was so mad, you could have fried eggs on my forehead. As I'm sputtering about my bad luck, Johnny says, "Look north, south, east, or west, up or down, and I guarantee you will find four places worse than where you presently are." I immediately realized he was right. Things could have been much worse. My ball wasn't in the water and I didn't have an unplayable lie. My anger evaporated. I made a good chip shot followed by a putt for par. Now I felt good again.

However, on the very next hole, I hit a bad drive and resumed my grumbling. After a second poor shot, I began launching my clubs into the stratosphere. If there were an Olympic event for golf-club chucking, I'd have qualified for the gold medal. Johnny watched this tirade with some amusement. As soon as I finished venting he said, "Lou, I play with all the world's greatest golfers, including Trevino, Palmer, and Nicklaus. I also watch them play each week on our TV broadcasts. I have seen you play seven holes today and I've got to tell you something: You aren't good enough to get mad. You are just a bad golfer. The minute you understand that you will enjoy your game for what it is." Was that a humbling assessment. But you know what? I couldn't argue with him. I was an adequate golfer, nothing more. Though my game hasn't improved much, I haven't lost my temper on a course since that day. When I hit a bad shot now, I say to myself, "Gee, I wish I was good enough to get mad, but unfortunately I'm not." My goal is to someday be skilled enough with my clubs that I can feel entitled to an outburst when my ball doesn't drop in. Somehow, I doubt that day is coming anytime soon. But I won't let frustration stand in the way of my enjoyment. I won't let adversity keep me from having fun. You might not be able to overcome every shortcoming, so learn to live with it and enjoy life.

Orange Bowl, 1977

I can never think of the victories my teams have attained without also considering the difficulties we had to overcome. In 1977—my first year at the University of Arkansas—our 10–1 record earned us an Orange Bowl bid to play the University of Oklahoma. It was obvious we would receive that invitation provided we beat SMU, which we did by a wide margin. Every time we scored against SMU, as we did often that afternoon, our fans littered the field with oranges. After the game, when the press asked what I thought of the display, I commented, "I'm glad we weren't going to the Gator Bowl."

A December 20 scrimmage was part of our Orange Bowl

preparation. Our team looked confident, solid at very position; I was certain it could whip anybody. My assistants and I decided to show them the scrimmage films on the twenty-first, then send everyone home for Christmas.

Before we could, Santa's elves brought us a package of trouble. Three players who had accounted for 78 percent of our touchdowns recklessly violated our Do Right rule, which governs personal conduct. I had to suspend them for the Orange Bowl. These were not bad guys; they simply made a bad decision. They chose not to play when they decided to behave badly. Now I had to support that choice. All three went to court to seek an injunction against my action. Fortunately, my attorney—you may have heard of him, his name is Bill Clinton—trumped all the arguments for their side. The suspensions stood.

So we scored a big win in the courtroom, but few doubted we could repeat it on the football field. Our fans and the media assumed the suspensions would decimate our offense and morale beyond healing. Three days before the Orange Bowl, we were 24-point underdogs. Then the game was taken off the boards. Journalists and TV commentators around the country were openly wondering about the commitment of our remaining players. I issued a statement that the suspensions would not be rescinded and that I expected our team to play an excellent game against Oklahoma.

Within thirty-six hours of my comments, I discovered I might not have a team. The attorney representing the suspended players called me and said, "Twelve of your best players aren't going to play in the game unless you lift the suspensions." I immediately issued a second statement that read, "Nineteen of our best players may not play in this game. I'm sorry to hear this, but I have always encouraged our athletes to think for themselves. If they don't want to represent the

University of Arkansas and people in this state against Oklahoma—a team we haven't played in fifty years and the last time we did they beat us 106–0—that is their prerogative. However, we are going to go play anyway and we plan on playing well."

Now the media had already heard from the boycotting players' lawyer that twelve of them were threatening to sit out the game. Naturally, when I met with reporters, the first question they asked was, "You said nineteen players. Their attorney is claiming only twelve. Which number is correct?" I replied, "I don't know, but it sounds like they must be losing support." That ended their boycott. When the striking players saw that discrepancy in the numbers—which is precisely why I inflated my claim in our press release—they were convinced that their teammates were defecting from the cause. No one ever wants to be the last man standing; you make too good a target. So they returned to us en masse.

Our team traveled to Miami the following day to prepare for the game. Anyone watching our practices could see that we were troubled. Our players were listless and unfocused. You might have said they were underconfident, but that would have implied that they had any confidence at all. They looked like a team that believed it could not win.

On December 29, I called together our players for a meeting. Once they assembled, you could feel the negativity in the room. There is usually a lot of banter and joking before we start, but everybody was somber that night. They just sat slumped in their chairs with their eyes glazed as if they'd just walked away from a car crash. I've seen livelier catatonics.

We began the meeting by admitting we were underdogs, but that I still expected them to win. I told them that just because the press was writing our obituary didn't mean we were obligated to die. Then I said, "Look, we've read all the reasons why we can't win. I want to hear why we can." At first, no one volunteered an opinion.

I told the team we weren't leaving until I got some answers. Slowly, they began to emphasize our positives. For example, one player pointed out that even though we had lost the majority of our offense, our defense was still intact and it was ranked first in the country. It was hard to score points against us, so there was no way we were going to get beaten as badly as the experts were predicting.

That got us rolling. Another player raised his hand and said, "We still have a powerful offensive line as well as the best punter and place kicker in the country." Then everyone conceded that Ron Calcagni, our quarterback, was a terrific competitor who could elevate any team. Of course, I kept hoping someone would point out what a great head coach we had. Somehow, that particular asset was never mentioned.

The more the players talked, the more positive they became. When we left that meeting, the team's persona had transformed. I almost felt sorry for our opponents. Our team wasn't merely ready to play, we were ready to win. Four days later, we beat Oklahoma 31–6. Running back Roland Sales gained a mind-boggling 205 yards to set what was then an Orange Bowl record.

It wasn't great coaching or strategy that carried the day. We won that game the moment our group of young men focused on what we had instead of what we lacked. That's the only perspective you can take in hard times. Remember that adversity presents us with numerous possibilities for success, if we are just willing to see them.

You Are What You Think

Winner and losers aren't born; they are the products of how they think. You never hear about mothers giving birth to lawyers, doctors, scientists, ministers, or bank presidents. They give birth to sons and daughters. What those individuals become is a matter of the choices they make. You ultimately decide whether you succeed or not.

We cannot pay people to win. The Chicago Bulls give Michael Jordan $33 million a year with the expectation that he will lead his team to a championship. But compensation does not guarantee performance. You must possess something inside of yourself that eschews mediocrity while embracing greatness. You must welcome adversity as a test of your resolve.

If Life Is a Classroom, Adversity Is Its Teacher

Every adverse incident in my life has taught me a valuable lesson. For example, after graduating from Kent State University, then finishing my hitch as an army lieutenant, I faced a dilemma. University of Iowa football coach Forest Evashevski, a friend of my college coach Trevor Reese, offered me a graduate assistantship for Iowa's 1960 season. At the same time, Coach Earl Bierderman of nearby Conneaut High School wanted me as his offensive backfield coordinator.

I had a big decision to make. I had recently proposed to a young lady from East Liverpool, Ohio, named Beth Barcus. She had accepted. So the choice I made would impact two lives. After weighing both job offers carefully, I decided to join Bierderman at Conneaut. Boy, did I think my life was set! I was marrying a terrific woman and taking a job in a field I loved. What could possibly go wrong?

Try everything. In the middle of July, Beth called off our wedding by informing me that she wanted to date other people. I was devastated by the news. Beth broke up with me at 9:00 P.M. By 11:00 that same night, I knew I couldn't hang around for that job at Conneaut. I packed my bags, got into my old 1952 Ford, and headed toward Iowa to accept Evashevski's offer. When I got into my car, I had no idea how to get to Iowa nor was I certain that the Ford could make the entire trip. I only knew one thing for sure: I was going to get as far away from town as fast as I possibly could.

A terrific first year at Iowa helped soothe some of my personal pain and disappointment. Coach Evashevski had assembled a talented football team that season; we would finish second nationally. I learned much about college coaching that year and knew I had discovered my vocation. Coach retired after the season. His successor, Jerry Burns, offered me an opportunity to join his staff as a full-time assistant. But Beth and I had reconciled by then. We had set another wedding date and Coach Burns didn't want me as his assistant if I was married. He felt my ability as a gopher, the guy who would go for this or go for that, was my best asset. Married men, he believed, did not make good gophers.

I couldn't find any work and was faced with unemployment. Jerry Burns rescued me by convincing Matt Drewer, head coach and athletic director of the College of William and Mary, to hire me as his backfield coach.

I stayed at William and Mary for three years until Coach Drewer retired to accept a bank presidency. The college selection committee narrowed its search for his successor to two candidates: twenty-six-year-old Lou Holtz and veteran college coach Marv Levy. That committee chose wisely. Coach Levy did an outstanding job at William and Mary. His success there catapulted him to his position as head coach of the Buffalo Bills. Before retiring from that post in 1997, Marv compiled one of the most impressive winning records in NFL history; he is a certain future Hall of Famer.

I moved on to the University of Connecticut as assistant to

Rick Fortano. Beth and I had two children by then, with a third on the way. Perhaps it was the increasing domestic obligations that led me to question myself and my future; I was no longer certain I could be a successful football coach. Beth and I discussed my options. We decided I could do one of three things:

1. Go to law school to become an attorney.

2. Get my doctorate in history and become a college professor.

3. Remain in coaching.

We agreed that since I loved it so much, I would remain in coaching for five more years. If things didn't pan out, I would still have plenty of time at thirty-two for other lucrative pursuits.

Our commitment was soon tested. I accepted a job as an assistant coach under Marvin Bass at the University of South Carolina. I was fired from that position in 1966 after Bass resigned and the new coach brought in his own staff. With a family to support and no immediate job prospects, things could not have appeared bleaker. But I never wallowed in self-pity. Didn't have the time. Instead, I focused on doing everything I could to find employment. Not long after, Woody Hayes, Ohio State University's resident football sage, offered me a position as one of his assistants. Everywhere I worked, I learned a little bit more about the game of football, life, and people. Eventually, I returned to the College of William and Mary in July 1969 to accept my first head coaching position.

We just reviewed my job history to drive home a point— catastrophes often disguise blessings. Beth's breakup with me felt like a death blow. Yet if she hadn't postponed our wedding, I might still be a high school football coach. Adversity pushed me toward the University of Iowa, where I started to prove myself in the collegiate ranks.

When we finally did marry, I had to give up my position at Iowa. A tough choice. But I persevered to find something even better at William and Mary. My pride was wounded when Marv Levy won that school's head coaching job. And once again, I needed a job. So what happens? I get an opportunity to earn my "post graduate degree" in coaching under a football legend, Woody Hayes. We won a National Championship at Ohio State. More important, Coach Hayes prepared me for a life devoted to football. Looking back, I realize that I didn't get the William and Mary job the first time around because I wasn't ready for it. Had the committee selected me instead of Levy, I would have failed. By the time I succeeded Marv at William and Mary, I knew I could do the job. All this demonstrates that things have a way of working themselves out if we just remain positive.

Mr. Johnson Didn't Listen

When you have people like Anthony Johnson on your team, good things often happen. Before coming to Notre Dame, this young man from South Bend, Indiana, was not a high school football star; in fact, he was only the third leading ground gainer on his high school team. Notre Dame rarely recruits athletes with such a relatively unimpressive résumé. However, we gave Anthony a scholarship because he was a tremendous leader who demonstrated great enthusiasm for the game of football. He was completely unselfish. Anthony started for us as a freshman and gave us four productive years. He was even elected captain of our team.

The Indianapolis Colts of the NFL drafted him out of college. He gave them two good years before he was cut. Did he quit after the Colts dropped him? No. He felt he could still play, so he engineered a tryout with the Chicago Bears. Anthony made the club, played well for another two years, then once again found himself unemployed. So he caught on with the New York Jets. And again he was cut after only two years.

You know what they say about three strikes and you're out. But this wasn't a baseball game and Anthony was never a quitter. There were plenty of people around the league who were saying he was finished. Anthony never heard them. He auditioned for the Carolina Panthers and won a starting job. Last season, Mr. Johnson was the club's leading ground gainer as he rushed for over 1,000 yards. Anthony has triumphed because he refused to believe it when three NFL coaches told him he wasn't good enough to play in their league. You see, it wasn't important what the coaches, general managers, or scouts thought about Anthony's ability. All that mattered was what Anthony thought.

Up from Adversity: The Making of a Team

When I first joined Notre Dame, I told our players, "We are not going to win because you have a new head coach, any more than you are going to fix a flat tire by changing the driver. We will win the minute all of us get rid of excuses as to why we can't win and stop wallowing in self-pity."

Our first game came against the number-two ranked University of Michigan. We outplayed them throughout four quarters; our team accumulated more than 500 yards in total offense that afternoon. Yet we lost, 24–23. A referee mistakenly ruled one of our touchdown passes was caught out of the end zone and our kicker missed a sure field goal on the game's last play. We came that close to winning. In the locker room, nearly every player had an excuse for our failure; there was a lot of finger-pointing that afternoon. My players seemed to have forgotten that whenever you point your finger at someone, three fingers point back at you.

We met Michigan State the following week on their home field. During the game's final minutes, with Michigan leading by 5, we drove the ball deep into their territory. I signaled for a time out and brought the team to the sideline. With a chance to win, I called for a pass play: 324, SxP. Those numbers don't mean anything to you, do they? What a coincidence. They didn't mean anything to my quarterback, either. He took the snap, stepped back into the pocket, and rifled a beautiful pass. Right into the arms of the Michigan safety. Interception. We lost the game 20–15. For the second consecutive week, we dropped a game we should have won.

Penn State, who would win the National Championship that season, played us in our eighth game of the season. In this contest, we proved how close we were to becoming a winning team. Our team made misplays at the most inopportune times (of course, the talented Penn State team had something to do with that). We also committed a number of foolish penalties (which told me we could still find a way to lose). During the game's last minute, one of our receivers dropped what should have been a game-winning touchdown pass in the end zone. Despite the miscues, Penn State only beat us by 5 points, 24–19. Still, I was distressed, not so much by the losses as by the players' general attitude. The inspirational verse, "I am only one, but I am one; I can't do everything, but I can do something; what I can do, I ought to do, and by the grace of God, I will do," didn't seem to have any place in our team philosophy.

It was a frustrating first year for me and my family. Each loss brought fresh criticism of my coaching skills. My son Skip's presence on our team made the situation even more difficult. I know it was distressing for him to hear the continual grievances against his father. I did everything I could think of to turn us around, but nothing seemed to work. Every week we played just well enough to lose to one of our country's most powerful college football teams. For example, when we met number-five-ranked LSU in Baton Rouge, we played them tough for all four quarters. So what happened? They beat us by two points, 21–19.

Southern Cal was our final opponent that season. We played them on their home field. This was a first-class team; they would eventually play Auburn in the Citrus Bowl. In the game's third quarter, we were down 30–20 with nine minutes left in the quarter. Southern Cal had the ball at midfield, a fourth-down situation with 5 yards to go. They opted to punt.

I felt we had a chance to stage an upset if we could just block the punt. We missed our attempt, but the play wasn't a complete loss. We did manage to rough the punter. For those of you who don't follow the game too closely, that's a no-no. We were hit with a devastating penalty that kept SC on offense in excellent field position. To make things worse, guess which player committed this faux pas? That's right, it was my wife's son, Skip (he was *our* son until the moment he collided with that punter). Former Notre Dame football coach Ara Parseghian was doing the TV commentary when the referee called the penalty. He said, "I wonder where Skip will live from now on." That was a bit much. I wouldn't throw my son out of our home for making a mistake in a mere game. I did, however, begin to understand the wisdom of animals who devour their young.

Southern Cal took advantage of our misplay to score yet another touchdown. They made the extra point to increase their lead to 37–20. We played evenly for the rest of the quarter and part of the fourth, which was not good news. With only nine minutes left in the game, we were down by 17 points. Skip, sitting on our bench distraught, was looking over applications for the French Foreign Legion. Our team mascot sat next to him, writing a suicide note. Ninety thousand fans were letting us know at the top of their lungs what losers we were. What really depressed me was that a lot of them were Notre Dame rooters. If there was ever a moment for a team to lay down, this was it.

What a time for a miracle!

Maybe it was the fans' taunts that did it. Or perhaps this team had just finally had enough of the excuses and the embarrassments. Enough of the losing. Because on what could have been one of the longest afternoons in my coaching career, this group of individuals banded together to form a team.

You could see this dramatic transformation on the sidelines. With the score still 37–20, our kickoff return unit made a commitment to get our offense into good field position. They made good on that promise; our offense took immediate advantage by scoring a touchdown. Then our offense urged the defense to keep SC off the scoreboard. This was no subtle thing. Our players were cheering each other on in a way I hadn't seen since joining the team.

Notre Dame's crisp defense stymied Southern Cal through a series of plays. After our offense literally roared out onto the field to score another TD, we held SC scoreless again. Then our punt returner Tim Brown carried the ball well into SC territory to set up a John Carney field goal. That was all we needed. Final score: Notre Dame 38, Southern Cal 37. We had outscored the opposition 18–0 during the game's last nine minutes.

As the final whistle sounded, our players turned the middle of the playing field into a joyous mosh pit. They hugged and leaped onto one another in a pile. We found a camaraderie that afternoon, a spirit of togetherness that remained with us for the rest of my coaching tenure. The losing was over. Our teams would win more than 80 percent of its games from that point on.

After landing his invasion forces on the shores of some country, the sixteenth-century Spanish conquistador Hernán Cortes would immediately burn his own boats. He was sending his army a message: "We can't turn back. Either we succeed here or we die here." Excuses were not an option.

Successful organizations have low alibi thresholds. They either do or they don't. Once you stop wasting energy fabricating excuses, you can start spending energy creating victories. The next time things aren't going your way and you're tempted to whine or finger-point, remember the words of the wise captain who said, "People don't care how rocky the ocean is, they just want you to bring the ship in." In other words, no one is interested in excuses, only results.

Come Together: A Remedy for Adversity

In 1993, Notre Dame opened its season with a convincing victory over Northwestern. We were preparing to play the following week's opponent—an excellent University of Michigan team—when a book titled *Under the Tarnished Dome* was released. I have not read this book and never intend to. I'd been told that it painted a negative image of me, Notre Dame, and the football program. (Fans who are upset with me occasionally send me a copy. They should save the postage, because I gleefully drop-kick it into the wastepaper basket without opening the cover.)

I had expected the book to be negative as soon as I learned

the identity of its author. This writer had first approached me with an idea for doing a book on Notre Dame football in 1987. He requested unfettered access to our Notre Dame family. For a variety of reasons—most of them concerning team policies—I turned him down. Naturally, the writer wasn't happy with my ruling. Too bad. I like to help people, but I don't coach to win popularity contests. I base my football decisions on what is best for the team's welfare. When I heard he had done a book on his own, I assumed it would disparage me and the school.

Amidst great publicity, Simon & Schuster released the book just as we were preparing to play Michigan. The national media reported some of the writer's more sensational accusations throughout the week. Everything I heard indicated that the book represented an unfair, inaccurate evaluation of our football program. Most of the athletes quoted in the book later wrote or called to tell me that they had been misled and misquoted. One player told me the author swore that his book would offer a favorable look at Notre Dame football. However, after the player told him of his positive experiences at Notre Dame, the author asked, "Did you have a drug problem on the team?" The young man answered no. Then the author said, "Surely somebody on the team must have been taking steroids." Since you can never be 100 percent sure of anything, the player responded, "Well, somebody *might* have been taking them." An innocuous enough answer, but the author reframed it as an outright admission that Notre Dame players used steroids.

The writer's accusations were widely reported. Members of the news media overran our campus. They dogged players and students for their reactions to the book. Even Ted Koppel devoted an edition of *Nightline* to the controversy. Ted is a fair journalist and he personally invited me to come on the show to offer my side of the Notre Dame story. I told him I had far more important things to do, such as preparing our team to play Michigan.

This was standard policy for me. When you are in the public limelight, you expect to be a target. You can't waste your time and energy hurling back every brickbat that someone tosses at you. I have always tried to consider my critic's side whenever they voiced their disapproval. If I recognized some validity in their comments, I did whatever I could to fix the problem. But if I felt the criticism was unwarranted, I generally ignored it. This left me open to additional attacks, but I felt it was the best way to handle the situation.

As the controversy heightened, I was concerned about the impact it could have on our players. Adversity can divide or coalesce. As it was, few people were impressed with our team that year. Even before *Under the Tarnished Dome* was published, many journalists had predicted we were on the verge of a losing season. Perhaps they were right. But I believe that book provided us with some much needed glue. Our players rallied together to give each other strength; we became a closer unit than we had ever been before. The students at Notre Dame also let me, my family, and the team know we had their full support.

We entered that game versus Michigan as the underdog. Oddsmakers were certain we would be too distracted and upset to bring any focus to the football field. They didn't realize our men had something to prove. We beat Michigan, 27–23. The team spirit that had been kindled by adversity carried us through a rousing season that ended with Notre Dame holding the number-two spot in the national rankings.

I'm Not Perfect: The Coach Misses an Opportunity

I have always felt that, in addition to the National Championship we won in 1988, we also should have taken top honors in

1989 and 1993. I don't care what criteria you use to evaluate the National Championship, we had a legitimate claim to the title in both years. I was disappointed that the media—who annually vote for the champion at the end of each season—didn't share my view. But hey, that's football.

I was upset, though, when I discovered that certain members of the media had cheered in the press box when they learned Notre Dame had lost a critical game. These journalists were supposed to be impartial. When I heard that story, I thought their bias toward Notre Dame probably cost us some votes. I should not have let it bother me. Instead, I should have used the slights to motivate our team to come back even stronger the following year. I didn't. I have to accept the blame for not channeling our frustration into something more productive. You can't allow difficulties to sink you. Everybody has problems. What separates the champions from the also-rans is how they react to them.

Fourth Becomes First

During my second year as head coach at William and Mary, we had four quarterbacks; three of them thought they should be first team. We settled on Jimmy Laycock as our starter. Our second-string quarterback didn't agree with our selection. He threatened to leave the team unless we gave him the job. It's never a good idea to blackmail the coach. He was gone by our second game. Shortly after his departure, a knee injury ended Jimmy's season. This meant we had to play the rest of the year with Bubba Hooker, our number-three passer, as our starting quarterback.

Bubba was our athletic director's son. He was a skillful passer and a willing competitor, but third string is still third string. Only a strange set of circumstances cast him in his starting role. Bubba performed well in his first game, a victory for us. Though we lost his next start against the Citadel, Bubba did throw two touchdown passes. Unfortunately, they were both interceptions to Jeff Varnadoe, the Citadel's premier defensive back.

This was a disastrous loss made worse when we discovered afterward that Bubba had broken his hand in the first quarter. Doctors said he would be lost to the team for the entire year. Chuck Clauson, one of our assistant coaches, tried to cheer me by recalling how his college team had suffered similar crippling injuries but still pulled off a National Championship. I thought to myself, "Sure, that's because you had a quarterback. We have nobody left who can throw the ball."

Our only option at QB was the most unlikely football player you've ever seen. He made me look like Arnold Schwarzenegger. Steve Reagan stood 5'8", weighed 154 pounds, wore high-top shoes, and ran the 40 in about three days. His father was a high school coach in East New Jersey and Stevie was only on a half scholarship. I remember when I first saw him on the field, I thought, "If he has to play, we are in big trouble!" Steve threw a decent pass, but that was the only physical skill he had to recommend him. However, he did possess an array of intangibles. Steve was button-tough, smart, unselfish, and a ferocious competitor. He hungered to play. Despite his laudable attitude, when he took over as quarterback, I thought we were done.

So much for my devotion to positive thinking.

Fortunately, Stevie didn't share his coach's pessimism. He proved to be the perfect catalyst for our team. Stevie led us to the Southern Conference Championship. We didn't lose a game with him as our quarterback until Toledo beat us in the Tangerine Bowl. He was our MVP. Funny, isn't it? I never would have played Stevie if injuries hadn't forced me to.

His performance taught me a valuable lesson: Never evaluate an individual by appearance alone. It also taught me we should never use our shortcomings as an excuse for failure. Stevie did not have great size, speed, or native ability. But he was too busy winning to notice all the things he lacked.

The Bad Times Are Relative

While I coached at Notre Dame, more players made the NFL from our school than from any other college. Obviously, we had good athletes who were physically talented. However, I also felt that our assistant coaches did a first-rate job of developing the players' fundamentals; a thorough grounding in the basics enhanced their chances of playing and surviving in the pros.

But perhaps the best thing we did to aid our players' development was to instill strong, positive attitudes that enabled them to succeed on campus, in life, or in the NFL, CIA, FBI, AAW, or any other acronym you care to name. Having the proper attitude helped them to develop good, consistent work habits and gave them the strength to handle adversity. These qualities are assets anywhere. As I have told our football team on those occasions when things were going against us: "Don't get discouraged. Someday, you are going to be thirty-one years old with three or four kids. One day you'll wake up to discover that the bank has just foreclosed on your mortgage and that your wife has run off with some drummer. But you won't blink an eye, because what we're encountering now is teaching you how to survive hard times. Handling adversity is part of life."

You know, it's amazing how that little chat never fails to cheer the boys up.

And a Blind Man Shall Lead Us

All of us should adopt the attitude of the blind man who was being led down the street by a guide dog. When they came to the corner of a busy intersection, the dog crossed against the light. The blind man had no choice but to follow. Cars swerved to avoid them; drivers honked their horns and swore loudly. Somehow, the duo reached the other side unharmed. As they stopped on the corner, the blind man reached into his pocket, pulled out a dog biscuit, and offered it to the reckless canine. Having just watched the two as they crossed, a bystander tapped the blind man on the shoulder and said, "Sir, that dog almost got you killed. The last thing you should do is give him a biscuit as a reward." The blind man smiled and said, "I'm not giving him a reward. I'm trying to find his mouth so I can kick him in the rear."

Whenever you find yourself moaning about some difficulty, remember that blind man. Give adversity a swift kick in the rear end. Drop the self-pity, throw out the crutches, trash the excuses. Do something positive. Welcome the most daunting challenges like a modern Cyrano de Bergerac. In Hooker's translation of the Edmond Rostand classic verse, the Comte de Guiche, in reference to Don Quixote, reminds Cyrano that "windmills, if you fight them, may swing around their huge arms and cast you down into the mire." A defiant Cyrano immediately responds, "Or lift you up among the stars!"

3

PUT THE WHY BEFORE THE WHERE OR WHAT: SENSE OF PURPOSE

I did not produce a winner with the New York Jets because I didn't persist. I left the job after only eight months because I had come to it without a clear sense of purpose. Sure, I wanted to win the Super Bowl. What NFL coach doesn't? But the New York media frenzy clouded my focus. No one's fault but my own. I couldn't provide the club with the direction it needed. I did benefit from the experience; I learned a lot about myself and the game I love. But I let down Mr. Hess, the club owner; Al Ward, his general manager; and the entire Jets organization. Absent a focus of my own, I couldn't give one to the club. I was embarrassed by my inability to provide the team with proper leadership. So I left. That one still eats at me. If I were coaching a pro team today, I would come to the job with one objective: to win the Super Bowl.

All winning teams are goal-oriented. Observe the San Francisco 49ers, the Green Bay Packers, the Dallas Cowboys. Teams like these win consistently because everyone connected with them concentrates on specific objectives. They go about their business with blinders on; nothing will distract them from achieving their aims. Losing teams lack focus. They are usually composed of individuals who act only on behalf of their own agendas, even if these are at cross-purposes with the goals of their colleagues and organizations.

If Everyone Cared

In June 1987, former baseball commissioner Peter Ueberroth spoke during my son Skip's graduation ceremonies at Notre Dame. The most memorable part of his speech came when he said we could accomplish anything in this world, solve any problem, if just enough people cared. I could not agree more. I have always felt that every football team I coached would be outstanding if only enough people on the team genuinely cared about our success. When you care passionately about anything, it gives you a sense of purpose. You won't let anything deter you from achieving your dream. This is true in virtually every area of your life.

Solve Before You Can Sell

When I was an assistant coach at the College of William and Mary, it was only a nine-month job. And it paid like one. To support my family, I had to find employment during the other three months. So during the summer of 1963, I got a job—selling cemetery plots. You want to talk about a difficult profession. When you sell cemetery plots, trust me, no one is eager to see you. How can you put a positive spin on a sales pitch for a grave? My wife, who is usually the most supportive person I know, tried to dissuade me from accepting the job. "You won't sell anything," she insisted.

Her words frustrated and motivated me. I worked my tail off all summer to prove her wrong. You should have seen me sell. I sold our radio, our TV, our sofa, our easy chair, I sold every piece of furniture we didn't need. I had to, because I couldn't sell a single cemetery plot!

My performance was such a disaster that my employers sent me to a two-day selling seminar in Richmond, Virginia. On the second day, one of the presenters, a fellow with a rep as a super salesman, announced, "I have a simple philosophy for selling." This immediately got my attention. Not being the brightest guy on the planet, I prefer to keep everything simple.

The salesman continued, "You don't *sell* anything. All you are trying to do is to help people get what they want. If you help enough people get what they want, you will eventually get what you want." He continued to point out that there wasn't a single successful business in this world that wasn't completely focused on satisfying its customers' needs. His talk was as illuminating as a searchlight. To sell anyone anything, he insisted, you have to forget whatever *you* want. Find out what the person on the opposite side of the table desires and give that to them.

That approach is still valid today. In his national best-seller, *Swim with the Sharks Without Being Eaten Alive,* Harvey Mackay poses sixty-six questions that you must answer affirmatively if you want to succeed in business. For me, his last question is the most significant one: "Do you know as much about your customer as your competitor does?" In essence, Harvey is saying the same thing that super salesman said to us more than thirty-five years ago. If you are in sales remember: You aren't selling anything, you are merely trying to solve your customers' problems better than anyone else can.

Say It Loud (And Proud): I Sell!

It bothers me whenever salespersons apologize for their choice of employment. I say to them, Stand up, pound your chest, and shout to the world that you are a salesperson and proud of it. Selling is a noble profession. You are the backbone of your country's commerce. You move products throughout the world and your efforts create jobs. You are bringing people what they want. For example, if you are an insurance salesperson, you aren't selling insurance. You are giving your customers security. I can't think of a more worthwhile endeavor.

Fulfilling a Need, Filling Your Wallet

How would you like to be the person who invents the next Wite-Out or Velcro? Try to figure out what the public needs and give it to them. It is much easier to fill a demand than to create one. Products enjoy longevity when they become an indispensable part of consumers' lives. Take a look at such fads as the Hula Hoop or Pet Rock. They each had their fifteen minutes of fame, but would you buy stock in a company built around either product today? On the other hand, such items as telephones, televisions, and computers sell perpetually. Once people have them, they can't live without them.

Marketing can accomplish a lot. But don't confuse the sizzle with the steak. You can hire a Ph.D. to drape your business and products with all the latest buzzwords, but if your merchandise doesn't perform, you won't last. Never forget whom you are there to serve. In school, we don't have students because we have a faculty. We have a faculty because we have students, coaches because we have players. You have an enterprise because you have customers. Lose them and you don't have anything. Slipshod performances on the playing field are usually due to a lack of focus. Don't lose yours. Always keep in mind that pleasing your customer is your primary objective.

The Impatient Shopper

I recently entered a store and stood behind four other customers. Even though a trio of different clerks were employed behind the counter, they were not waiting on any of us. Oblivious to anything else, all three were involved in a personal discussion. It was only after they sensed our restlessness that they gave us any attention at all. Even then, they didn't do it cheerfully. They acted as if we were encroaching on their social lives.

After making my purchase, I asked to see the manager. Suddenly, my clerk was magically transformed. He was all smiles and glad hands. He said, "I'm sorry if I kept you waiting." I smiled back and said, "Don't worry, it won't happen again. I can assure you it won't." That sounded like a threat only because it was. It was obvious that these employees did not appreciate how their livelihoods depended on their customers. Anyone who owns or manages an enterprise should ensure that their employees understand this. With the hope that no one will have to wait so long for service again, I put together the following list of customer service reminders. Feel free to post it in some prominent place in the office or on the selling floor:

What Our Customers Mean to Us

Customers are the most important people in our business.

Customers do not depend on us, we depend on them.

Customer never interrupt our work, they are our work.

Customers do us a favor when they call; we don't do them favors by letting them in.

Customers are part of our business, not outsiders.

Customers are flesh-and-blood human beings, not cold statistics.

Customers bring us their wants; we fulfill them.

Customers are not to be argued with.

Customers deserve courteous attention.

Customers are the lifeblood of this and every other business.

Customers are who we are when we're not working (So let's treat them the way we want to be treated ourselves!).

All these guidelines are saying the same thing: Concentrate on the customer. You can't make many catches if you take your eyes off the ball.

What Might Have Been: Lunch Under the Golden Arches

In 1959, I was an army lieutenant stationed in Fort Knox, Kentucky. One day, I headed to Louisville on a weekend pass to search for some R&R (rest and rehabilitation, for you civilians). I drove my car down Dixie Dieway (as the military called it) until I saw this restaurant with golden arches that advertised a complete meal—hamburgers, fries, and a Coke—for thirty-five cents. It was my first McDonald's.

Price was important to me back then; I was only making $212 a month. So the idea of paying less than half a buck for lunch had a particular appeal. I didn't expect much for such a small amount of money, but I was pleasantly surprised. The food was hot, tasty, and served in a jiffy. The restaurant was immaculate. I had never seen anything quite like this in East Liverpool, Ohio. I had never seen or eaten in a fast-food restaurant before. It was special. I knew by the way everyone there went about their business that the franchise was going to be a winner. These employees knew what their customers wanted and they made sure they got it.

As I was sitting in the McDonald's parking lot, preparing to leave, I thought, "Lou Holtz, you are not going to go into coaching, you are going to open a McDonald's restaurant in East Liverpool." How could it miss? As I made this career-altering decision, I looked up at the McDonald's sign and noticed something that discouraged me. It read, "Over 1 million served." I said to myself, "It's too late. I should have gotten in on the ground floor." This was forty years ago, and since then McDonald's has served billions of hamburgers. This organization expanded beyond anything I could have imagined by focusing on its niche customers and answering their needs.

The Little Business That Could: U.S. Filter

McDonald's is only one of many thousands of businesses that have dominated their market by making customer satisfaction their primary objective. Another example of a company that has done this is U.S. Filter. In 1991, they did approximately $17 million in business. Six years later, they are approaching *$3 billion!* Why? Because its management never makes a decision without first considering its customers.

Dick Heckman is the visionary who leads the company. I recently asked him why he entered this business and what he saw as its future. Dick revealed that he started the company to *answer a desperate need*. He had read enough to know that the world is facing a health crisis. Clean unfiltered water—once considered so abundant we took it for granted—is rapidly becoming a rare commodity. Its supply is diminishing while the demand for it is increasing. Our present water systems' decaying infrastructures exacerbate the problem.

I'm not sure if you realize the health hazard posed by pollution. I certainly had no idea until Dick told me that contaminated water caused 10 million worldwide deaths annually. Impure water is behind four out of five of the globe's most common diseases. In the United States alone, the most technologically advanced country on earth, 50 million people are exposed to contaminated water daily.

As we all know, water is one of life's essentials. Since we cannot produce more unless we find a way to control climate—an unlikely event—Dick realized we had to conserve and purify the supply we have. He founded U.S. Filter to do exactly that. Talk about answering a need! That is the reason this company has enjoyed such an astounding success. Everyone involved with this business is driven by a common purpose: to satisfy our customers' water needs. That is all they focus on, so they are continually refining and improving their systems. Mortgage America, located in Bay City, Michigan, is another company built on its founder's sense of purpose. Tom LaPorte started this business with a laudable sense of purpose: He wanted to make mortgages accessible to people whom the banks had turned down. Why? Because Tom believes that homeowners give a community strength and permanence. Mortgage America isn't just a business for him, it's a mission. Which is why it has been such an extraordinary success.

When you earn even a small bit of fame, companies that want you to endorse their products will form a line outside your home. I've turned down nearly every one of them. But I've associated myself with companies like U.S. Filter and Mortgage America because they have demonstrated the vigor, foresight, and determination common to all championship teams. Both companies have concentrated on goals that go beyond mere profits. You shouldn't give your time to any enterprise without demanding the same.

Think Team All the Time

Getting everyone on your team pointed in the same direction is the most difficult challenge any coach faces. What is a football coach's primary objective? To guide his players to All-American honors or positions in the NFL? No, those are individual accomplishments that should be the byproduct rather than the goal of genuine teamwork. We are on the field and in the locker room to teach our players how to win. Not just on the gridiron, but in any profession they choose. We want to impart work habits that will lead them to excellence throughout their lives. Most of all, we want to teach them the value of loyalty, integrity, and teamwork. Once you learn how to work with people, you can accomplish anything. To do this, you must subvert your ego in the service of a higher cause. You must never forget that there is no "I" in the word "team."

Because I believe that, I never put names on the backs of our players' jerseys. At Notre Dame, we believed the interlocking ND was all the identification you needed. Whenever anyone complained, I told them they were lucky we allowed numbers on the uniforms. Given my druthers, I would have nothing more than initials indicating what position the wearer played. If your priority is the team rather than yourself, what else do you need?

Instilling freshmen with strong team spirit is never an easy chore. It has been my experience that most freshmen athletes are more concerned with their playing time than whether their team wins or losses. Sophomores are primarily interested in winning starting positions. The team could go 0–14, but if they are starting every week and making the plays, they're happy.

Juniors are different. They've established themselves on the team, expect to play, and are free to focus on winning. Seniors, however, are generally looking to next year. They are chiefly concerned with their future in football beyond the university. If they have demonstrated any talent at all, agents have probably already approached them. These agents fill the athletes' heads with visions of NFL glory and riches. Attaining these blandishments can become a player's chief objective, often to the detriment of the team. I believe most coaches don't trust or like agents because they can shift an athlete's focus from "us" to "I."

I always asked my players to refrain from hiring agents until the pro draft is completed. I also advise them to make the agents work for their money. For example, if I were a player drafted by the Dallas Cowboys, I would go to team owner Jerry Jones and say, "Make me your best offer." Let's say he offers me a $1 million signing bonus plus a four-year contract with a $500,000 annual salary (and if you're reading this, Jerry, and have this in mind, we can talk). I would show that offer to my agent and say, "This is what I earned on my own. I will pay you a percentage of everything you get beyond this, because that's what you will have earned."

Of course, hardly anyone ever takes my sage advice on any of these matters.

Every Wolf Needs a Pack

When I coached the North Carolina State Wolfpack, we had a saying: "The strength of the pack was in the wolf and the strength of the wolf was in the pack." I tried to carry that attitude over to every team I coached. No player on our Notre Dame team exemplified that more than Tony Rice. He was one of the greatest competitors I have ever been associated with. Mind you, he was not the most talented athlete I have ever coached, but he had a burning desire to win. A game we played against the University of Pittsburgh in 1988 will give you some idea of what I'm talking about.

We had been beating Pittsburgh for most of the afternoon. However, the Panthers scored late in the third quarter to tie us. Their hometown fans were going absolutely crazy. When I looked across the field, I could swear the Pitt players were striding eight feet off the ground. They had the look of eagles about them. When a team takes on that look, they are usually unstoppable. With a full quarter left in the game, I was concerned as we lined up to receive Pitt's kickoff.

Then Tony Rice approached me and said, "Boy, Coach, this is a great game, isn't it?" That tells you everything you need to know about Tony. He didn't want to bully some team in a blowout, he wanted a challenge! He simply loved to compete. And he always wanted to win. Tony could turn in a record-breaking performance in a game, but if we lost, you wouldn't see him smiling in the clubhouse. How many yards he accumulated were never his priority. All Tony Rice ever cared about was winning. When you have that strong a commitment, you transmit it to your entire team.

If you watched the University of Michigan's football team play during the 1997 season, you saw a team of Tony Rices. With the possible exception of Rob Woodson, the school didn't have a single superstar, someone whose stats made your eyes pop. Michigan's players exceeded everyone's expectations because they understood that the strength of the pack is in the wolf and the strength of the wolf is in the pack. They put a capital "T" in the word "team." Any business can learn from their example. You don't need a superstar performer on your roster to beat the competition. You just have to get everyone in your organization to contribute their best effort to a common cause. Our teams have had walk-ons, scrubs who were never going to see any significant amount of playing time. Yet they contributed enthusiasm to the team and this helped us win.

Meet Mr. Carter

If you would like another example of a person with his priorities in order, let me introduce you to Tommy Carter. I coached Tommy at Notre Dame. He is an outstanding defensive back—a first-round NFL pick—who currently plays for the Chicago Bears. After one particularly fine performance in which he led us to a big win, Tommy was the one player every journalist in our locker room wanted to interview. But no one could find him. They looked everywhere, but apparently the star of the game had vanished without talking to a single reporter.

One enterprising writer finally tracked him down. In the university library. After one of the greatest games of his college career, Tommy Carter wasn't taking time to accept the press's accolades or celebrate with his friends. He was studying. When asked why, Tommy explained that his roommate was playing in the dorm championship football game the following day; he wanted to go to the game to show his support. He couldn't do that unless he finished his studies for the weekend that night. Tommy loved football; he's made it his life's work. But he came to Notre Dame with an objective: to earn a diploma. He wasn't going to let anything deter him from that goal.

The Notre Dame Way

The University of Notre Dame commands respect throughout the world. The school's storied reputation isn't built on its football program (though that has made a sizable contribution to it). Educators, parents, and students hold Notre Dame in such high regard because of its dedication to an unwavering objective: to give its students the best education possible. This commitment extends beyond its classrooms. Notre Dame students not only learn how to earn livings, they also discover how to live. Any school that teaches you one without the other is only fulfilling half its obligation. If you are looking for a school for yourself or a loved one, choose an institution that builds character as well as careers.

Choices Are Easy . . . When You Know What You Want

You will never be indecisive if you know your purpose. Faced with a dilemma, the correct choice will reveal itself once you weigh your options against your objectives. These should be durable, long-term goals, otherwise you may be tempted to forsake them for the lure of instant gratification. For example, students may face a choice of carousing all night or studying for a big exam. If their primary objective is to get a diploma, then there really is no choice. They are obligated to themselves to crack open those books. However, if they are not sure what they want to accomplish in school and life—if they don't feel it in their bellies—they may very well waste the night in some small bar, and then waste the next day with one large regret.

Your Country, Your Self

I follow current events closely. I have great respect for most politicians, but when a problem occurs in Washington, it seems it's because someone forgot why the people elected them. I know there are many differing opinions on the role government should play in our lives. I'd like to suggest a way to resolve them. Let's look at the Constitution and ask ourselves why we even have a government? Why did we fight the War of Independence? What made this country great? What will make it greater in the future? We can't answer any of those questions until we know what we want this country to be. All of us must find some common objectives.

It's the same with life. You can't solve your personal issues until you define your purpose.

What are you trying to accomplish? What have you done today to bring you closer to your goals? The moment we lose sight of our objectives, we founder. We've all heard of church ministers who were banished by their flocks after committing an act of sexual misconduct, embezzlement, or some other malfeasance. I don't believe they would have erred so badly had they only remembered why they first took up their ministries. If they were committed to leading people to God, you know they wouldn't make such horrendous choices.

I serve on the board of directors of America's Promise— The Alliance for Youth. General Colin Powell is our chairman. He is among the most impressive people I've ever met. He has a commanding presence and exudes determination. You just know if you give this man a task, it is going to get done. You only have to stand next to him for a few minutes to understand why Desert Storm was such a triumph. Most generals come from upper income families who could afford to send them to private schools. General Powell rose up from a relatively poor neighborhood. He had a public school education. This background was not a disadvantage, because Colin Powell is a man of purpose. His life teaches us that we can rise to elite levels if we keep our eyes on the prize.

Whatever Gets You There

Anyone who knows me realizes that I don't like to drive big, luxury automobiles; they are just not my style. When I was a boy, my dad always drove a big car; he thought people were impressed when they saw him behind the wheel. Father only had a third-grade education and he needed something to buttress his confidence. He was a fine man and I loved him very much. But I was never comfortable with his choice of automobiles. We probably had the biggest car on the block, but there was never enough money to repair it or keep it filled with gasoline.

When I buy an automobile, I don't look for something pricey with a lot of size and flash. Once my children wanted me to purchase a fancy sports car; I chose a bland model without any frills. I think it was a hot color though, kind of a deep beige. The kids razzed me about this, so I asked them, "That car you wanted me to buy, does it fly? Can you drive it in water? Will it drive itself? Do you have to put gasoline in it? All that big, fancy automobile can do is get me from point A to point B just like my little car." I was letting them know that I didn't derive my self-esteem from some material object. To me, a car has one purpose—to get you where you're going. I choose a vehicle that meets my objective. All our decisions should be based on the same criterion.

Presently, we are building an addition to our home. Every married couple should do this before their divorce becomes final. Watching the workmen lay the foundation reminded me of the story about the three bricklayers who were asked what they were doing. The first responded, "I am laying bricks." The second said, "I am making $17.50 an hour." The third said, "I'm building the most beautiful cathedral in town. Years from now people will be able to come here and worship." Which individual do you think understood his sense of purpose? Which one do you think brought more to his job?

4

GETTING GAME-READY: MAKE SACRIFICE YOUR ALLY

Have you ever walked into a class knowing you were inadequately prepared? Isn't it one of the worst feelings in the world? I remember speaking with Dr. Roberts, my college history professor, prior to taking an exam I hadn't studied for. I told him, "I sure *hope* I do well on that quiz today." That was my subtle way of saying, "I haven't cracked open a book, don't know Napoleon from Josephine, but I don't want to fail. So would you *please* exercise some charity when you grade my paper?" Dr. Roberts got the message. He threw me a soul-withering look and said, "The time to worry, son, is before you place your bet, not after they spin the wheel." Sound advice. When you put in the time, you don't have to fret over the results.

Winners Don't Gripe

Success never comes easily. I have inherited five losing football teams during my coaching career. If you asked me if these squads had anything in common, I would say yes. They were all largely composed of athletes who moaned about everything. You cannot turn around teams like that unless you rehabilitate the malcontents or sweep them from their rosters.

To excel, our college players had to attend classes, train, and play unselfishly. They also had to adhere to curfews and other regulations that were never applied to the average student. Superior players don't complain about such restrictions, they take pride in them. They understand their willingness to sacrifice places them among that rare breed of individuals who will do whatever is necessary to attain their goals.

When a difficult task comes your way, accept the challenge joyfully. Once it is finished, plead for more. Every sacrifice you make builds character. People with average skills often obtain greatness because they are willing to pay a price for it. You might not be able to outthink, outmarket, or outspend your competition, but you can outwork them.

Sorry I Asked, Padre

Can you think of better role models for discipline and sacrifice than the Trappist monks? They are renowned for their vows of silence. Try not talking for just a day and see how much self-restraint it takes. My attitude toward gripers is summed up in the story about the Trappist monk who was allowed to say only two words every three years. After the first three years, he met with the his order's Brother Superior and said, "Bad bed!" Three years later, he came back to say, "Bad food!" After three more years of silence, the monk said, "No TV!" Another three years passed. This time, when the monk met with Brother Superior, he handed him his robes and sandals and announced, "I quit!" Brother Superior said, "Well don't expect me to try to dissuade you. You've done nothing but complain since you got here!"

A Gift from My Mother

My parents gave me this respect for sacrifice. I was able to go to college because Mother earned my tuition while working from 11:00 P.M. to 7:00 A.M. as a nurse's aide. This was a cause for her. No one on either side of our family had ever gone to university before; my mother was proud that I was the first. So she was willing to make sacrifices if it meant I could enjoy a better life.

It was a trying time. My younger sister was still living at home and needed parental guidance. Mother couldn't shirk that responsibility simply because she was working the graveyard shift. Dad pitched in, but Mom still had to perform a variety of roles—nurse's aide, mother, and wife—on little sleep. This was an act of deep, abiding love.

Marriage entails sacrifice. I believe you should enter it with the idea that there is no way out once you are in. Marriages work best when each party is committed to the other's happiness and success. You will often have to give up something if you are to uphold your end of that bargain.

Raising children also requires sacrifice. When you have a child, you suddenly realize that you are no longer free to do whatever you want, whenever you want. Your child's welfare and happiness become your top priority.

For example, when I was an assistant coach at the College of William and Mary, my young family struggled to keep a positive balance in our checking account. There were few things we could afford. We had one car, an eleven-year-old jalopy so banged up I would leave the keys in it hoping someone would swipe it. There was no chance of that. Who would want to risk going to jail over that wreck? Of course, I also knew that if they did steal it, they wouldn't be able to go very far. The world's most neurotic rock star never suffered as many breakdowns as that automobile. We didn't worry about burglars, either. One look at our few modest belongings and they probably would have taken up a collection for us.

Obviously, we were tightly budgeted. But when our children begged us to take them to *Disney on Parade*, we scraped together the money. Sure, my wife and I missed a few lunches. But what price can you put on your child's smile? It's easy to make sacrifices such as these when you have your priorities in order.

Boudreau Was Ready

While I was watching the Cleveland Indians play the Florida Marlins during the 1997 World Series, I found myself reminiscing about the great Cleveland baseball teams of my youth. I was an Indians fanatic as a youngster. Even today, I can name the starting lineups for both their 1948 world champion team and the 1954 club, which still holds the AL record for most wins in a season.

As I recall, the 1948 Indians played Detroit in their season's final contest. Cleveland entered the action in first place, but their lead over the second-place Boston Red Sox was a mere game. Boston was scheduled to play its finale against the New York Yankees that same afternoon. If the Indians could beat Detroit, they would clinch the American League pennant no matter what Boston did. If Cleveland and Boston both lost, the Indians would still take the flag. However, if Boston won while the Indians lost, the Red Sox would force a one-game playoff on their home field, Fenway Park—where Boston rarely lost.

I listened to the Indians-Tigers matchup on the radio. My team entered the bottom of the ninth losing, 2–1. Throughout the season, Cleveland's shortstop/manager Lou Boudreau had been the team's clutch performer. It seemed as if every time his club needed a big hit or defensive play, Boudreau was there. He performed a miracle every day, no two miracles alike. His performance that season was so scintillating that it would win him the American League's Most Valuable Player Award. I was certain he would produce some last-inning heroics to pull out this victory as well. But this wasn't to be Lou's or the Indians' day. Detroit hung a loss on them. Of course, the BoSox beat the Yankees, so now Cleveland faced a sudden-death match on their enemy's turf.

Everyone who rooted for Cleveland was counting on Boudreau to put Boston away once and for all. He had been "the man" all season, so naturally there was a lot of pressure on him to again work his magic. Did the expectations of his fans and the media unnerve Boudreau? Not so you could tell. With the pennant at stake, Boudreau played his best game of the season. The Indians triumphed and went on to win the World Series in five games against the Boston Braves.

You will only succumb to stress if you are ill-prepared. Boudreau excelled under pressure because of the sacrifices he had made throughout his career. All the hours spent in the batting cage, all the ground balls he had taken in practice, had readied him for the most crucial moment of his career. You can be just as cool and productive as this MVP was in any situation if you approach your life with similar dedication.

Chris Zorich, Role Model

I introduced you to Chris Zorich in our first chapter. He was the young man who was so distraught in the Notre Dame locker room after we lost the Cotton Bowl. Chris is an exceptional individual. He came from a broken family. His father—whom Chris never met—was black, his mother white. She raised her son in a downtrodden Chicago neighborhood that had been battered by drugs and crime. Chris had to literally fight his way home from school every day. He grew up amidst a bleak landscape of muggings, rapes, homicides, robberies . . . every heinous crime you could possibly imagine.

Chris was a good though not great high school athlete. He arrived at Notre Dame thinking of himself as a starting linebacker. I knew that wasn't his position the moment I saw him run. He wasn't quite fast enough. However, I did think Chris's talents were suitable for middle guard. He was devastated when I recommended the shift. Chris even contemplated transferring to another school, but decided against it.

Freshman year wasn't kind to Mr. Zorich. He played little and struggled with his studies. But there was no surrender in him. Chris worked hard to improve. He had no social life to speak of. When he wasn't on the practice field or in the weight room, he was hunkered down with his books. I don't believe I ever saw him when he wasn't doing something to improve himself. And on the field, he never gave less than his all. Chris played football with the kind of fervor that is shared by everyone who attains greatness.

Chris not only molded himself into a crackerjack middle guard, he eventually became captain of our National Championship team. When we won the Orange Bowl, the sportswriters voted him the game's outstanding defensive player. They also named him to the All-American team his senior year. Despite all these accolades, Chris will tell you he earned his greatest honor off the field: a diploma from the University of Notre Dame.

When Chris graduated, scouts insisted he was too small to

play professional ball. I guess no one ever told them it's not the size of the player in the fight but the size of the fight in the player that counts. Instead of being discouraged by their evaluation, Chris devoted himself to a rigorous training program that increased his power and speed. He has established himself as a starter with the Chicago Bears of the National Football League.

The city of Chicago has bestowed many awards on Chris for his tireless efforts on behalf of the underprivileged. He raises money year-round for his charitable foundation and is involved in countless other causes. One of Chris's favorite projects is to provide Thanksgiving and Christmas dinners for numerous poverty-stricken youngsters. We should all applaud Chris and others like him. Too many people aren't willing to make sacrifices to help themselves, let alone others. Chris has done both, as an athlete and a benefactor. I believe one of the reasons he is so compassionate is that he has never forgotten what it's like to struggle. The sacrifices you make should motivate you while they enhance your self-esteem. But they should also keep you humble. They should keep your heart open and alive to the pain of others.

The No-Bonus Bowl

At the time I joined North Carolina State as head football coach, the team had won only three games in three years. You would think any team could win more often than that just by accident. However, I walked into a wonderful situation with that school. We had several outstanding athletes returning from the previous season. All they had needed for their skills to ripen was some game experience. Once they had that, the administration could have named Homer Simpson to lead these men. North Carolina State was going to start winning again no matter who coached them. I was just fortunate to be there when the wheel came around. In my four years at the school, we earned four consecutive Bowl bids.

My first season with North Carolina State was probably my most rewarding as a coach. No one expected us to do much, but we started winning immediately. We capped a great comeback year by beating West Virginia in the Peach Bowl. It was a fairy-tale season.

Two weeks after our Bowl victory, I visited Willis Casey, our athletic director. Willis was short on words but long on common sense. After discussing our prospects for next season with him, I said, "Willis, this is probably an oversight on your part, but you haven't mentioned anything to me about the Bowl bonuses for the assistant coaches and me." Willis's eyes went cold. Peering over his glasses, he asked, "What bonuses?" I replied, "Well, we did take our team to a Bowl. Our fans filled the stadium to capacity for every game. We played regularly on national TV, which helped increase the contributions from our alumni and supporters. When a team does all that, the school usually rewards the head coach and his assistants with a month's salary." I finished my soliloquy by reminding him of the outstanding work our assistants had done all year. Not one of them ever shirked an assignment, and the extra hours they had put in had ensured that every facet of our game was honed to perfection.

As I pointed out, what I was requesting was not uncommon. At most of the schools in our conference, such bonus agreements were standard policy. In fact, I doubt there was a major football program in the entire country that didn't reward its coaches for earning a Bowl bid.

Willis, however, had a different perspective. He looked me in the eye and said, "I want to tell you something: I *hired* you to do all these things. Why do you think I fired the last coach?

Because he didn't do them. So please don't request a bonus for doing the job you were hired to do. Now, is there anything else you wish to talk about?" I said, "No, sir," and immediately left. Willis's cool, reasoned response had made quite an impression on me. He was absolutely right. I was employed to build a winning football program, but like too many other people, I wanted additional compensation for doing nothing more than my job. When you are hired by an organization, don't expect them to tear up your contract and pay you extra for the sacrifices you make to achieve excellence. That's what they hired you to do! If they give you a bonus, give them your thanks. But always remember that you initially accepted their salary in exchange for your promise to deliver your maximum effort. You owe them nothing less.

Students Who Can Teach Us All Something

I have boundless esteem for the students of Notre Dame. Most of those I've met are witty, clever, and successful. I remember the first game I ever coached at the university. We started the morning with a glorious team mass, then walked as a group toward our stadium to play arch-rival Michigan. As we passed through the campus, I saw a sheet hanging on the ivy-covered wall of a nearby dorm. You couldn't miss this thing. It covered nearly the entire wall and must have been forty feet high. At the top, it read, "John 3:16." The punch line appeared right under that: "Lou, 12–0." I thought some students' expectations might have been a tad high, but each year I coached at South Bend, we tried to come as close to that perfect mark as we could.

Every student who attends Notre Dame must make some sacrifices. Tuition there is expensive and the school's standards are high. You don't have too much time for a varied nightlife (if you do, you're grades are probably in the rear of the pack). I thought the social whirl at Notre Dame was best summed up by Todd Lyght, our All-American defensive back and team captain, when he stood up at a team luncheon and said, "I wish to discuss my experiences here at Notre Dame. Let me start with my social life first." He paused for a long, utterly silent moment, then said, "Now that I have covered that phase of the Notre Dame experience, let's move on to my academic record." The audience broke up with knowing laughter.

I am sure many Notre Dame students could have made that same speech. But I'm also certain they would tell you any sacrifice they made seemed infinitesimally small when compared to the size of the rewards they reaped. And I'm not just talking about the diplomas they earned. They left the world's most prestigious learning institution with friends they could count on forever as well as values that would see them right throughout their lives.

Notre Dame's climate also forces its students and teachers to sacrifice. Unless you're an Eskimo or a polar bear, you've probably never experienced anything like it. South Bend, Indiana, is located just south of Lake Michigan. During the winter months, frigid gusts blow off the water, transforming everything into ice. It snows continually. The skies are often overcast. And those are the more clement days.

Weather played an important role in the school's founding. I am not sure if many people realize this, but South Bend was not the original choice to be Notre Dame's home. As I was told—probably after I initially complained about the region's sub-zero conditions—its founders wanted to locate the school in sunny, warm California. A group of five French priests, led by a Father Sorin, left Baltimore, Maryland, in 1842 bound for San Diego, where they intended to open the West Coast's first Catholic university. As they traveled across Northern Indiana, they found themselves in the midst of a monster blizzard. Powerful winds conspired with the pelting snow to drop the temperature below freezing. After slogging for hours without making any significant advance, Father Sorin supposedly said, "I can't go any farther. Let's set up camp here. We will resume our travels the moment the weather improves." If they were alive today, they'd still be waiting. That's why Notre Dame is in South Bend and not in San Diego. And that's also why I went almost a decade in between tans.

Always Look for an Edge

You may be asking why I think sacrifice is vital to any winning game plan. My answer is simple: So few people are willing to make them. Those of you who habitually do that little bit extra will enjoy a tremendous edge over your competition. For example, during the 1950s, there was a Lever Brothers salesman who thought about winning every waking hour. He made Saturdays part of his regular schedule because he knew rivals loathed working weekends. Since he was the only salesperson calling that day, owners were willing to give him more time to show his entire line. By calling only on small accounts on Saturday, he had more hours to spend with his larger accounts during the week.

People who are willing to sacrifice are quick to transform every negative into a positive. When a snowstorm hit his territory, this super salesman didn't see an obstacle when he looked out his window. He saw opportunity! Knowing that his competitors would be tucked in their homes hiding from the elements motivated him to pull on his boots and call on accounts. As he has said, "Business has always been a game for me. Every day was another chance to put some points on the board. Those other salesman were the opposition. I could have stayed home like them when it snowed or stormed, but that would have meant falling behind or settling for a tie score. That was never good enough for me. It shouldn't be good enough for anybody who wants to succeed."

The gentleman with that championship spirit is Mr. Victor Kiam. He worked himself up from a management trainee with Lever Brothers to become one of the most recognized entrepreneurs in the world. You know him as the high-profile owner of the Remington products, or "The Man Who Bought the Company." He has also owned over twenty other enterprises, including the New England Patriots of the National Football League. He has realized nearly every dream he's ever had because he was willing to pay a price in sweat and time. Make the same investment and you'll never finish second to anyone.

A Promise Kept

George Stewart was the first athlete I ever recruited for the University of Arkansas. He hailed from Parkview High School in Little Rock and was the most highly recruited athlete in the state. George had everything: speed, strength, coordination. A tremendous football player. He was also an excellent leader from an outstanding, tightly knit family. His parents valued education. When I recruited him, I promised both his folks I would do everything I could to ensure that George earned a diploma.

From the moment George joined our team, you could see why he was so sought-after. He would participate in our Orange Bowl win over Oklahoma though he was only a freshman. Before he was through, he made All-American and was elected team captain in his senior year. Unfortunately, a knee injury—suffered during training camp with the Kansas City Chiefs of the NFL—kept him from pursuing a professional football career. He went to work as a car salesman for Moore Ford and performed exceptionally.

Some months after he left our school, I received a phone call from George's mother. She wasn't happy. "You promised that our son would graduate from the University of Arkansas," she reminded me. "He hasn't. Don't you think you should do something about that?" What could I say? She was absolutely right. I immediately called George and tried to persuade him to return to campus to finish his degree.

Though he was only one semester shy of completing his requirements, George wasn't eager to come back to university. He said, "Coach, I really appreciate the call, but I earn a lot of money here and I enjoy what I do." I said, "George, that's fine, but you must get your degree. You are limiting your future if you don't. What will you do if you get tired of sales? Once you receive that diploma, there is absolutely no door that will be closed to you. I know we're asking you to make a sacrifice. It's hard to step away from that paycheck. But once you leave here, you'll be able to do anything you want, whether it be selling cars or coaching, whatever. And while you are getting your diploma, I want you to help our football team. I've already cleared this with the athletic department and the university. I think it's in your best interest." I was using the lure of a job in football as an arm twister. Like Don Corleone, I was trying to make him an offer he couldn't refuse. But if he turned me down, I didn't know what I would do. I mean, I didn't have any Luca Brasi's to send over as gentle persuaders.

Fortunately, I didn't need Luca. After mulling over what I said, George came back to school. He not only got his degree, he turned out to be a natural coach. He later accepted my invitation to join my staff at the University of Minnesota as a full-time assistant. George did an exemplary job at Minnesota. I took him to Notre Dame, where he helped us win the National Championship. He is now an assistant coach for the San Francisco 49ers, one of the most respected coaches in the country.

To fulfill his mother's dream, George had to give up his job as a salesman making a substantial salary. However, he is now involved with his true love, the great game of football. As a coach, George has helped many people reach their dreams. I'm sure he would tell you today that he has been amply repaid for the sacrifices he made to earn his degree.

Saving As Sacrifice

Every time you put a dollar in your savings account, you're making a sacrifice. My first big-time coaching job was as an assistant coach at the College of William and Mary. My salary was a staggering $5,900. This represented decent money in those days, but no one was confusing us with the Rockefellers. Though we met all of our bills, there was rarely much left over. My wife and I decided that we would invest 5 percent of every paycheck into a savings account. We pretended it was a bill and made it our first priority every month. To do this and still honor our other financial obligations, we had to give up some things. Was it easy? No. Was it worth it? Absolutely. We felt it was important to build a nest egg. With the money we saved, we were eventually able to buy a house and send our children to the colleges of their choice.

Any mention of sacrifice reminds me of the story told about the Ohio gentleman whose oil well caught fire. He put out an all-points bulletin for assistance. To ensure a heavy response, the oil baron also offered a $30,000 reward to whoever could quench the flames. All the large firehouses from Newell, Chester, East Liverpool, Wellsville, Salineville, and Dillonvale sent help. They dispatched their best companies, accompanied by their most modern fire-fighting equipment. However, not one of their trucks could get within 200 yards of the blaze. The heat was just too intense.

Finally, the Calcutta Township Volunteer Fire Department appeared on the scene. They had only one rickety truck equipped with a single ladder, two buckets of water, three buckets of sand, and a blanket. It didn't even come with a hose. When that old truck reached the point where all those other fire companies had stopped, its driver didn't hesitate. He kept barreling ahead until he and his crew were on top of the blaze. Calcutta's volunteers leapt out of the truck, threw the two buckets of water and three buckets of sand on the inferno, then beat the fire out with the blanket.

That oil man was so impressed by this display of courage, he gave the driver $30,000 in cash on the spot and asked, "What are you and your men going to do with all that money?" The driver didn't hesitate, replying, "The first thing we're going to do is get those gosh darn brakes on that truck fixed." The lesson here is that not all sacrifices are voluntary. Sometimes circumstances force us to make them. However, in the long run, we're grateful that we did.

Always Give Something More

When I was an assistant coach under Woody Hayes at Ohio State, we were scheduled to host a Purdue team that was, at the time, ranked number one nationally. The roster of this football juggernaut included Leroy Keys, a star running back, and Mike Phipps, one of the most talented college quarterbacks in the country. The rest of the team was nearly as impressive. Most experts were picking Purdue to win the Big Ten that year; many thought they were a cinch to take the National Championship. No one had to tell us how good they were. We had played them the previous season and gotten trounced.

This was going to be our biggest game of the year; it seemed as if everyone in Columbus was angling for seats. I knew many of my relatives and fraternity brothers were going to attend. No one who came out to watch us that day went away disappointed. Both teams put on a clinic in football defense throughout the first half. At the start of the third quarter, Ted Provost, our defensive cornerback, intercepted a Purdue pass and ran it back in for a touchdown to break open a 0–0 game. That was all we needed. We held our opponents scoreless for the rest of the afternoon, beating them 13–0 in a grand upset.

Being part of this extraordinary team effort was my greatest thrill as an assistant coach. We were nearly delirious with joy in our winning locker room. I couldn't wait to celebrate that evening with family and friends. But then reality intruded. I remembered that when you coached under Woody Hayes, you couldn't leave the stadium as soon as the game ended. You had to wait two hours until that afternoon's game film was developed, scrutinized, and evaluated.

Our coaching staff met that evening at 7:00. After viewing and grading the Purdue film, we started doing our homework for Michigan State, our opponent for the following week. Had Coach Hayes not required our presence, I wouldn't have been there. But Coach understood the value of sacrifice; he expected his assistants to share his dedication. The disciplined work habits we developed under him gave us a winning edge over those opponents who weren't willing to do a little bit extra. Sure, we lost some hours with our loved ones;

this was the price excellence demanded. You must be willing to pay it.

Let me leave you with the fable about the Emperor who years ago gathered together the wisest people in his kingdom and said, "I want you to assemble all the great knowledge of our civilization so that it is easily available for future generations." They worked many years before returning with ten bound volumes. His Highness glanced at the stack of books, frowned, and said, "Too long." The sages scurried from his throne room. They did not return until they had edited the ten volumes down to one. However, when they handed it to the Emperor, he refused to open it. "Still too lengthy," he said. Over the next two years, the sages condensed the book into one paragraph. The Emperor wasn't satisfied. Finally, these wise people came back with a single sentence inscribed on an index card. The Emperor read it, smiled, and announced, "This is perfect. Now future generations will understand why we have been so successful. All the genius we possess is contained in this brilliant, solitary, phrase."

The sentence read: "There is no free lunch." You can dine on Ken-L Ration or filet mignon; it all depends on how high a price you are willing to pay for the meal.

5

ADAPT OR DIE: THE PERILS OF BEING NUMBER ONE

Change is inevitable . . . unless you're using a vending machine. This is especially true in business. If you compared two lists of Fortune 500 companies—one from twenty years ago and one compiled today— you would be amazed at how few businesses appear on both tallies. Organizations fall out of favor when they fail to keep pace with their customers' changing needs. Once you reach an elite level of your profession, you must continually adapt to maintain or improve your position.

For example, in college football, quarterbacks are throwing the ball more often now than ever before. Scholarship numbers have declined and there are fewer coaches. When I first coached, we could practice as long as we wanted; now we're limited to twenty hours a week. You can't grumble about the changes or use them as excuses for losing. As long as the rules apply to everyone, you must adjust and excel.

Complacency is your enemy. When we became number one at the University of Notre Dame, I suddenly assumed that our touchdowns would count for 12 points instead of 6. If we fumbled, I expected the opposing team to wipe off the ball and hand it back to us. After all, we were number one. Weren't we entitled to some perks? Was I mistaken! When we became number one, our problems multiplied. We were a team of targets, and every Dirty Harry in the conference had his .44 Magnum aimed at our spines.

It is so much easier to hide among the pack instead of being the lead dog. When you are working toward that top spot, you are never satisfied. You are open to any changes that might improve your organization. You can evaluate yourself against the performance of whoever is running ahead of you.

When you finally reach number one, you're all alone. There's nobody left to chase. So there's a temptation not to run quite as fast as before. You forget that the time to shift into overdrive is when you are the hunted not the hunter. You have to show some extra foot so the competition doesn't gain on you.

The top perch in any field carries a weighty responsibility. Once you attain it, everyone expects you to dominate your competition; you are supposed to be the best. Should your customers discover that your product or service is short of dazzling, they will shop elsewhere. A competitor may get away with selling them an inferior product because the customers come to it with lowered expectations. If you're number one, no one will cut you that kind of slack.

So how can you survive at the summit? Raise your standards and expectations until they surpass your customers'. Now what will happen when you do that? Since nothing in business, sports, or life takes place in a vacuum, your competitors are going to respond. They will study your strengths and probe your weaknesses. They will emulate or improve upon anything you do right and exploit anything you do wrong. Your achievements should motivate everyone in your organization to step up their games, because they'll surely inspire your competition to do the same.

When you are number one, change becomes intimidating. Why alter the way you do business now? Everything is great. Then some calamity strikes—new technology renders your products obsolete or your market share declines rapidly—and forces you to modify. But change usually fails when it is a response to panic. Always remember that no matter how well things are going, you can always improve something. Making voluntary changes now saves you from being forced to make mandatory changes later. However, never alter anything simply for the sake of doing something different. Any modifications you attempt must have clear, productive goals.

"We're Not Holding Anything!"

When you sit at the top of your industry, you must resist the temptation to sit back on your success. Adopt the philosophy of General George Patton, who once told his troops, "I don't want any communiqués saying you are holding your position. We're not holding anything. We'll let the enemy try to do that. We are attacking day and night!" The time to start congratulating yourself for your accomplishments is when your task or career is over. In other words, don't pop open the champagne until the party starts. You still have much to achieve.

If you don't experience complacency at the top, you may feel anxiety. As I've said, when you are number one, everyone is gunning for you. The pressure to maintain your position can be crushing. Insecurities bubble to the top. Did you win because you were talented or merely lucky? There is always one thing you can do when the pressure pushes in on you. Dream bigger. Put your focus on where you are going rather than where you've been. That's one mistake I made at Notre Dame. After we were champions, I stopped dreaming. I'll never commit that error again.

You Can't Accomplish Anything Big Without Doing the Little Things

Organizations must be fundamentally sound if they are to endure change. Fundamentals form the cornerstone of your business. They are easy to ignore, because practicing the basics is often methodical and boring. However, in football you can have a roster full of players with exceptional skills, who can throw or pass with anyone. But if they don't pick up their assignments, or fail to block and tackle, you won't win many games. You may possess the world's most beautiful singing voice, but if you don't practice your breathing and projection techniques, you aren't going to be headlining at Carnegie Hall anytime soon. A company can produce the greatest product since sliced bread, but if its marketing program ignores the basics, who will buy it?

There will be times when you stumble and fall. However, if your fundamentals are in place, they will act as a safety net. Your fall will never be precipitous. And you will always bounce back up. Too often, businesspeople try to stop a downslide by making radical alterations in policy and strategy. Before doing that, examine the basics. Are you still doing the little things that made you successful in the first place. Good football teams can block and tackle, good students can read and write. If you can't execute the basics, you can't succeed.

Since I talk about them frequently, people often ask me, "What do you mean by 'fundamentals'?" I define them as all the small things that are essential to your success. Using that as a guide, compile a list of the tasks you must perform to meet your goals. Then meticulously perform those assignments day in, day out. Make alterations as you find out what works and what doesn't. If productivity declines, go back to your list. See if you're forgetting some small, vital step. Be consistent.

Fundamentals are basically doing the little things correctly. Players and coaches undoubtedly thought I was neurotic when I insisted that we look like a crack football team before the ball was snapped. I believed the way we aligned our feet in the huddle and got into our stance was integral to our success. When we practiced something as basic as our huddle, I wanted each player to have his hands on his knees and his heels straight. This focused everyone.

We also spent more time practicing our set position than other squads. And we kept everything simple. Our opponents would call the team to set with commands like "Blue . . . 982 . . . Virginia." First time I heard one of our quarterbacks yell out something like that, I thought, "Good Lord, no! We'll never be able to remember all that." So we changed it to "Set, hit," followed by a hand clap. If my players clapped in unison, we knew they were focused and synchronized. But if there was a ripple of clapping, we knew the team needed more practice. Our players found this exercise boring. They were right. But we did it every day. It was the primary reason officials rarely called offside penalties against our teams. I don't even want to think about how many close victories would have been close defeats if we hadn't practiced this maneuver so meticulously.

When you have to pay attention to how you enter and break from a huddle, how you line up, and other seemingly minor details, it carries over when you execute larger assignments. It also tells the opposition you are all business. That can be intimidating, especially to a competitor who lacks your professionalism. You can usually tell how a team is going to play just by observing how it goes about the basics. Whenever one of our opponents appeared to be misaligned in its huddle or on the line, I knew we were in for a long, grueling afternoon.

Whenever I stress the importance of fundamentals, I like to tell the story about the guy who walked into the pet shop to buy a bird. He noticed several of them were listed at $1.90. When he went to buy one, the pet store owner said, "You don't want those birds, sir. I have the ideal bird here for you and it's only $692." The guy looked at the bird and said, "Why it's just like all those other birds. How come it's so expensive?" The store owner replied, "Ah, but this bird is different. It can talk and sing. The other birds just sit there." The guy thought for a minute and said, "Gee, it's a lot of money, but I live alone and would love to have the company." So he bought the bird for $692. The next day the customer returned to the store, found the owner, and complained, "I paid $692 for that bird and it doesn't talk or sing." The owner said, "Well, sir, what did the bird do after he rang his bell?" The customer asked, "What bell?" The owner said, "The bell the bird rings to tune himself. If he can't tune himself, he can't talk or sing. I've got a bell here for only $23." So the customer purchased the bell.

He returned irate the next day and complained, "My bird rang the bell, but he still doesn't talk or sing." The owner replied, "That's impossible. I have the same type of bird as you. Why, just today he got up, rang the little bell, then ran up and down his ladder." The guy stopped him and said, "What ladder?" The owner said, "You mean to tell me that you didn't buy the ladder! That bird won't talk or sing unless he first gets his exercise on the ladder. We have a ladder on sale today for only $27." The guy bought the ladder. Over the next three days the storekeeper sold him a mirror, a swing, a bird bath, and a pecking tree. At the end of the week, the customer returned in tears. He told the storekeeper, "My bird finally talked this morning. He woke up, rang the bell, ran up and down the ladder, pecked his tree, swung on his swing, and keeled over in his bath. Just before he died, he looked over to me and said, 'Couldn't you buy any bird seed?'" Fundamentals. Ignore them at your peril.

"I Got All I Needed"

In 1981, our University of Arkansas team was playing a midseason game against the University of Texas. Our opponents were ranked first nationally; we were number twelve. Ours was a good team, but obviously not a great one. During pregame warmups, our players appeared sharp. You could see it by their meticulous approach to the basics. We ran Texas off the field that day. It was as fine a team performance as I have ever witnessed anywhere. Texas was our arch-rival, so our victory couldn't have been more exhilarating.

The day after our win, I received a phone call from Roy Kidd, the successful head coach of Eastern Kentucky. Everyone in our profession respects him tremendously, so I was flattered by his call. Roy said he had watched our team beat Texas and wanted to ask me about our huddle. I answered all of his questions. Just as our conversation drew to a close, I asked, "Roy, aren't you interested in anything we did offensively or defensively or how we motivated our team?" He said, "No, I got all I needed. Thank you for your time," and hung up the phone. That was seventeen years ago and I have never forgotten it. Roy was a coach's coach. He understood. Fundamentals are everything.

Do What You Love, Love What You Do

Enthusiasm. It's a word derived from the Greek, meaning "to be inspired by God." I've always associated it with success. Everybody has enthusiasm at one time or another in their life. Some people have it for thirty seconds, others for thirty years. The people who maintains it long-term will attain their goals. I've done a coach's show on TV throughout my career. I didn't particularly relish doing them at first. However, I made up my mind that I was going to have a great time whenever I went on the air, and I think people sensed that. The more I enjoyed myself with my guests, the higher our ratings climbed. Enthusiasm is contagious. If you have enthusiasm for what you do, people will want to share in it.

Mark Twain understood this. Remember when Tom Sawyer had to whitewash his Aunt Polly's fence. How he hated that chore! But he did it with a smile and soon convinced all his friends that nothing could be more fun. When they asked if they could join in, Tom hesitated. He made them think he was having such a good time he didn't want to share a minute of it. So what did they do? They each offered to pay him to let them take a turn with the brush. They were fighting among themselves to see who would go first. Tom's friends had caught his enthusiasm. It's amazing what a little fervor can do for any organization. If your salespeople love their products and transmit sparks when they make their presentations, customers are going to buy. But if they simply go through the motions, they won't get a single order.

For example, in Arkansas, I opened my TV show every week by saying, "Greetings, and welcome to the *Lou Holtz Show*. I'm Lou Holtz." I did it exactly the same way every week. One evening, though, after a disappointing loss, I said, "Greetings and welcome to the *Lou Holtz Show*. Unfortunately, I'm Lou Holtz." Killed everyone's enthusiasm before the first commercial. Our guests, our audience, even our crew were soon as down as I was. I've seen funerals that were more fun than that show and zombies who were livelier hosts. I never again opened with such a downbeat greeting.

Sometimes You Get the Bear, Most Times the Bear Gets You

Only you can change yourself. Don't expect your parents, spouse, colleagues, or friends to transform you. It's not their job. You can alter any aspect of your life once you accept that you are the product of your decisions. Continue to do whatever you've done before and the results will remain the same. Why shouldn't they? Revamp your approach to life and you will produce a different outcome.

When I was an assistant coach at the College of William and Mary, I had a sign on my desk that read "May God give me the courage to change the things I can, the serenity to accept the things I can't, and the wisdom to know the difference between the two." It was not a well-known saying at the time, but it has become widely quoted since. There *will* be some things you can't change. You can accept that provided you have tried your best. For example, following the 1979 season our Arkansas team played Bear Bryant's Alabama squad in the Sugar Bowl for the National Championship. We had a good football team; Alabama had a great one. Bear's Crimson Tide had been number one the previous year and had remained number one throughout the entire '79 season.

You should never let the competition awe you, so I suspected we were in trouble when I attended a pre–Sugar Bowl party. That's when I saw my players standing in line to get Coach Bryant's autograph. Despite that, we played a near-perfect game. Unfortunately, Alabama played flawlessly to beat us. As soon as the ref blew the final whistle, I walked over to the Alabama bench, shook Bear's hand, and said, "Coach, your team played a great game." He looked down at me—they didn't call him Bear because he was small—and drawled, "Lou, that's the best game we've played in five years." I replied, "Gee, I'm glad I had the chance to see it, Coach." I knew no matter how well we played that afternoon, we couldn't have beaten Alabama. I could have changed our game plan, changed our uniforms, heck, I could have changed teams and it wouldn't have made any difference. They had a more mature, confident, and talented club. When your best efforts fail, don't waste time thinking "what if." Close ranks, march on, and use the loss as a learning experience. Then go back and study your game films. Find out what you did wrong and where you can improve. Start planning to win your next game.

You Have to Wait and See

As you must know by now, I believe most problems are blessings in disguise. You can transform any tragedy into a positive experience simply by altering your perspective. We often cannot tell an obstruction from an opportunity until we view it from hindsight. So be patient.

Whenever I am tempted to judge a situation prematurely, I remember the story of John, a fellow who owned a valuable mare. One night the horse ran off and all the neighbors said, "John, we're so sorry your horse has disappeared." John replied, "I don't know if it's good or bad. We will have to wait and see." The next day everyone was shocked when the horse returned accompanied by two beautiful wild stallions. All the neighbors said, "Oh, John you are so lucky. You have three fine horses now!" John replied, "I don't know if it's good or bad. We will have to wait and see."

The following day, John's two sons were riding the new horses. Both boys suffered broken legs after being thrown. Everybody immediately cried, "Oh, John, that's too bad that both your sons broke their legs!" John replied, "I don't know if it's good or bad. We will have to wait and see." That weekend war broke out. All the able young men in the village were summoned into military service. All except John's sons. Their broken legs earned them 4-F deferments. Everyone declared, "Oh, John, that's good, your sons don't have to go to war." Once again, John replied. "I don't know if it's good or bad, we'll just have to wait and see."

This tale illustrates what I have discovered on numerous occasions: You can't classify anything as good or bad until all the results are in. When my fiancée ended our engagement, I was so crushed I had to immediately leave town. I couldn't bear the thought of running into her every day. So I took the job that began my college coaching career. And when Beth and I did reconcile, our union was stronger for our breakup. Every time I've lost a position, it gave me the opportunity to find something better. Don't be discouraged by setbacks. Remember, no matter what happens, you just have to wait and see.

Are You Cheating Your People?
Never Shortchange Anyone!

Soon after accepting the position of head football coach of North Carolina State, I attended the National Football Coaching Clinic in Chicago. I arrived late at my hotel, because I had been recruiting players throughout the region. Or trying to. Most of my prospects showed little interest in joining us. They were unimpressed by North Carolina State's recent mediocre record and the quality of its football program. I couldn't convince anyone that day that I was the man to turn things around. When I reached the hotel lobby, I was dejected as well as tired.

As I went to get my room key, I ran into a friend, Wayne Hardin, head football coach for Temple University. Wayne asked me to join him for a drink. As we talked, he asked me what I considered a strange question: "Lou, are you the best football coach in the country?" Since Woody Hayes, Bear Bryant, and a hundred other fine coaches were still stalking the planet, I had to answer truthfully. "No," I replied, "but I want to be." Wayne said, "Well, then you're stealing NC State's money and you should resign. They hired you because they think you *are* the best coach in the country for that job. For you to say anything less is a disservice to your employer."

Few conversations have ever cost me any sleep; that one did. After a night's reflection, I concluded that Wayne was right. If the university thought I was the best man to coach its team, then my performance had to match those expectations. This should be your attitude whenever you accept a job. Someone hired you because they believe you have more talent than anyone else who applied for your position. Reward the confidence they have placed in you. Think as highly of yourself as your employer does. When problems arise, don't complain. You were hired to solve them.

Like the Song Says, "You Can't Please Everyone, So You've Got to Please Yourself"

If your happiness depends on your pleasing other people, you are going to have one unhappy life. When I first came to Notre Dame, I was told that our alumni would be satisfied with me as long as I kept the team competitive. I knew it would be a challenge, since the football program had some obvious problems. In the final game of the previous season, Miami had trounced Notre Dame, 58–6. And that was only the worst of the discouraging losses the team had absorbed that year. So no one was particularly optimistic when I arrived in South Bend.

During that first season, we lost six games, five of them by a total of 14 points to teams that finished in the national Top 15. Despite the mediocre win-loss record, I thought we had been competitive in every contest. The alums put me straight in a hurry. "You don't understand," they told me, "being competitive at Notre Dame doesn't mean coming close. It means winning."

During my second year, we had one of the best records in the country, a winning percentage that should have sated everyone's appetite for victory. Obviously, I still didn't get it. You see, even though we had made it all the way to the Cotton Bowl, we didn't win the National Championship. "When we say win," the alums explained, "we mean win it all!"

That's exactly what we did in our third year. Was everybody happy? No! A number of them complained, "We meant win by a big score! Dominate!" Hearing that, I concluded you cannot satisfy everyone. You are always going to encounter people who have unrealistic expectations. Funny thing, though. These people rarely place the same demands on themselves that they do on others. They are often the types who won't put up but can't shut up. You'll go insane trying to please them, so don't even bother.

That Word—Failure

The first motivational book I ever read was *The Magic of Thinking Big*, by David Schwartz. Several chapters addressed the dynamics of failure, leading me to examine how we react to setbacks. I have observed people who are so frustrated by failure, they abandon their fundamentals. They forget about doing the basics that have brought them success in the past. It doesn't occur to them that the problem may not lie in what they are doing, but how they are doing it.

When they can't pinpoint a reason for their failure (probably because they aren't looking in the right place), they feel victimized. "Why," they ask, "is this happening to me?" They may become verbally or physically aggressive as a means of venting their resentment. You see these people all the time. They start fistfights over parking spaces or some other trivial matter. If the failure continues, their insecurity increases. They begin doubting their decisions. Before long, they abdicate any leadership positions they hold. To keep in mind all negative aspects of failure, I have turned the word into an acronym:

F   Frustration (You don't have any answers.)

A   Aggression (Misdirected.)

I   Insecurity (You can't cut it anymore.)

L   Leadership (You abandon it.)

U   Undisciplined (You stop practicing fundamentals.)

R   Resentment (You assume the victim's role.)

E   Excuses (It's everyone's fault but your own.)

How can you prevent failure from undermining you? By remembering that the person who doesn't fail is the person who doesn't attempt anything. Understand that failure is inevitable; see it as part of your learning process. When things go poorly, review your fundamentals. Are you leaving out any steps, taking any shortcuts? Whenever officials dropped a lot of yellow penalty flags on one of our teams, I knew we were ignoring some basics. So we put even greater emphasis on them at our next practice.

Are you questioning your ability? Don't. You've performed well in the past; you'll do so again in the future. Your talent isn't a tangible object. No one can steal it from you (although you can fritter it away). However, you should evaluate your performance to see if you must make any adjustments to adapt to changing conditions. For instance, if our quarter-back's arm didn't have its usual bounce, we might call more running plays or short-yardage passes until it revived.

No matter how frustrated you get during rough times, don't take it out on others. You need allies. Show character. Don't blame anyone for your mistakes. Rather than dwell on your losses, focus on your assets. Do these things and any failure you encounter will be temporary.

Of course, you have to discover what your problem is. Don't be like the fellow who woke up feeling like one big wound. He immediately went to his doctor's office and said, "Doctor, everywhere I touch it hurts. I touch my left shoulder it hurts. I touch my right shoulder it hurts. I touch my leg it hurts. I touch my head it hurts. I touch my chest it hurts. I touch my foot it hurts. Everywhere I touch it hurts. Am I dying?" After a thorough examination, the doctor said, "You have a broken index finger."

That patient is a good example of someone who should have followed the KISS rule: Keep It Simple, Stupid. Before searching for complex solutions to your troubles, try to see the obvious. That isn't always easy. You might need a dispassionate party to point it out to you. Whenever I give that advice I am reminded of the two guys, John and Mike, who were sitting in Murphy's Bar. Mike looked at John and said,

"You look familiar." John said, "You do, too. Where are you from?" Mike replied, "Dublin, Ireland." John said, "That's amazing, I'm from Dublin, too." So Mike asked, "What part of Dublin?" And John replied, "The Northwest side."

Mike was flabbergasted. He exclaimed, "I'm from the Northwest side. What school did you attend?" John said, "St. Mary's." Of course, Mike had gone there as well. As they continued to speak, they learned that both had graduated in 1991. Mike downed his beer in one gulp. "This is all too incredible. Let me ask you. Where did you live?" John replied, "Foley Avenue." "Saints alive," cried Mike, "that's where I live." Just then another guy walked into the bar to order a drink from the owner. "What's new Murph?" the customer inquired. Pointing a thumb toward the two brothers, Murph responded, "Oh, the same old thing. The O'Brien twins are drunk again."

Don't be like the O'Brien boys. Always remember that the solution you seek is often directly in front of you.

Do Your Job!

In 1970, I coached William and Mary in our season opener against West Virginia. The game was played on their home field in Morgantown. This was an exciting day for me. I was born in Follansbee, West Virginia, and grew up in East Liverpool, Ohio, which is only a long punt from Morgantown. I got tickets for virtually everyone I knew. We packed the stadium. My parents, grandparents, aunts, and uncles were all there. Wow, what a thrill when we walked out on that field! As the cheers embraced me, I thought I was the luckiest fellow in the world.

If that was so, my luck didn't hold out for long. West Virginia took the opening kickoff and immediately drove for a touchdown. The game wasn't fifteen seconds old and we were already losing by seven. Going into the contest, I had liked our chances, even though I knew West Virginia had two great backs, Braxton and Grisham, who were NFL bound. Once we took the field against them, though, I knew they were just too big, strong, and well-coached for us to win. But I didn't want to get drubbed in front of my family and friends.

Despite our opponents' opening blitzkrieg, I had good reason to believe we would not be embarrassed. West Virginia head coach Bobby Bowden was a close friend of mine. He had too much class to run up the score against me in front of my hometown fans. Our team played its heart out. With one and a half minutes left in the game, we were losing 34–7. Then, with West Virginia's first team still in the game, Braxton scored a touchdown in the closing seconds to make the final 41–7.

Looking back, I realize the final score was meaningless. As that great football aficionado Gertrude Stein once noted, "A loss is a loss is a loss." But at the time, I was piqued that Bobby had run up the score against us. He didn't have to keep his first team on the gridiron after it had sealed the win. When we met at mid-field, I said, "Bobby, I thought we were friends. How could you let your team keep piling on points like that in front of my family." Bobby calmly replied, "Lou, it's your job to keep the score down, not mine. You can only coach one football team and that's yours. You can't coach yours and mine. If you don't want to get beat badly, get better athletes, coach better, or change the schedule."

Bobby was right, and his advice was some of the best I've ever received. Remember, if you have a problem, it's your problem. Solve it. Don't blame other people. Don't burden people with your complaints. Ninety percent of the people you meet don't care about your troubles. The other 10 percent are glad you have them.

Be Flexible Enough to Adjust

Many times you must change your plan in mid-game. For example, in 1987 Notre Dame traveled to Pittsburgh to play the Panthers. We found ourselves down 26–0. Compounding our troubles, we lost starting quarterback Terry Andrysiak for the rest of the season when he suffered an injury on the last play of the first half.

We had to make several offensive modifications during halftime. This was imperative. Our new quarterback, Tony Rice, had a radically different style from Andrysiak. However, the biggest change we needed to effect was an attitude shift. You cannot win unless you believe you can win. When your team is behind 26–0, its easy to entertain some doubts. We had to eliminate those before we again took the field.

I called the team together and said, "We have been a fine offensive football team all season. Even though we have a new, inexperienced quarterback, I don't think we should have any difficulty scoring two touchdowns during the second half, particularly since we have averaged well over thirty points a game." I then explained what I expected to score with our kicking game. Given what we had achieved up until then, the numbers seemed reasonable. I also requested that our defense set up one touchdown. Again, not an impossible task.

Then I asked our players, "Can we keep any team from scoring for just two quarters?" Everyone knew we could. I told them, "That means all we need to win is two touchdowns from our offense, one from our defense, and one from our kicking game." Well, there wasn't anyone in the locker room who didn't think we could do that.

As it happened, our offense did score 20 points and the kicking game set up another TD. However, our defense let us down. It not only failed to get its touchdown, it allowed the Panthers to score again. So we lost by a narrow margin, which goes to prove that not every locker room talk results in a victory. Sometimes, you lose one for the Gipper. But we proved to ourselves that we could adapt and come back. We won our next five games in a row to enjoy a fine season. The changes that we were forced to make proved to be beneficial in the long run.

Periodically, I will say the following: "I am not what I want to be, I am not what I ought to be, I am not what I am going to be, but thank God, I am not what I used to be." I then ask myself, "Is the latter true in my case?" As long as we are changing for the better, we have a chance to succeed. Any changes you make should be positive. With that in mind, I'd like to close this chapter with a saying I learned from a nun in grade school. She would have us recite:

Good, better, best,
Never, never rest,
'til the good is better,
and the better is best.

Not bad words to live by, are they?

6

RUN FOR DAYLIGHT: COMPETING ON YOUR FIELD OF DREAMS

Here's a puzzler: More Americans than ever before are jogging, lifting weights, bicycling, speed-walking, playing racquetball, practicing yoga, and trying anything else that will keep them fit. Yet fatigue is a national malady. Many people feel too worn down to go all out; they simply don't have the energy to give life their best shots. What's causing this malaise? I think boredom is the culprit. You can swallow vitamins by the bottleful, but unless you add a dose of enthusiasm, you won't have the strength to grab life with both hands. As a means of countering your chronic fatigue, Dr. Holtz recommends that you find something to engage your passions. Start living your dreams. Whatever you choose, it should propel you out of bed every morning hungry to accomplish something.

That Vision Thing

Every great accomplishment I've ever heard of started with someone's dream. What is a visionary if not a dreamer?

Dr. Martin Luther King was certainly a visionary. He didn't see the world as it was, but dreamed of it as it could be. What would the reaction have been had he stood before that throng of 500,000 in Washington, D.C., and shouted, "I have a strategic plan!" Who would have noticed? However, when he declared, "I have a dream!" souls were stirred and our society began changing for the better.

Carl Pohlad's Fountain of Youth

Carl Pohlad is one of Minnesota's most successful citizens. He has owned the Minnesota Twins baseball team and has been a winner at everything he's tried. Carl looks like a young fifty, but that's impossible, since the last time I saw him he was celebrating his Golden Wedding Anniversary. Carl is at least seventy-five, but you wouldn't know it from being around him. He loves to participate in sports, particularly golf, and is active in the ongoing business of all his holdings. He wakes up every day alive to new opportunities. When I attended his anniversary, he asked me to say hello to his mom. That good lady is well over one hundred and has more vitality than many teenagers of my acquaintance. What's her secret? Like her son, she stays interested in the world around her. She's a participant in her own life, not a spectator. I keep reading about people taking vitamin supplements, herbs, shark oils, and other concoctions to prolong their lives. Proper nutrition does play a role in longevity and I'm all for it. But if you want to prolong your life, spend less time popping vitamin capsules and reading health magazines and more time living.

I've always believed that dreams make the best chauffeurs, because they will drive you anywhere you want to go. Dreamers positively seethe with youthful excitement no matter what their age. I've seen eighty-year-olds with teenage eyes sparkling with hope and expectation. They attack each day, foraging every hour for adventure, challenge, and opportunity. Then, sadly there are the twenty-year-olds I've seen with eyes as lifeless as tombstones. My guess is that some naysayers have brutalized these young people by denying them their right to dream. We can help them heal by encouraging them to live large lives filled with challenges so that they rise each morning thinking, "Every day someone accomplishes the impossible. Today, that someone will be me!"

Hey, If I Can Do It . . .

I can certainly provide anyone with ample evidence that the most ordinary person is capable of living an extraordinary life. I have always been physically unimpressive. As a high school student, I must have established the longest losing streak in the recorded history of dating. We're not just talking about a string of bad dates, I mean I didn't go on dates at all. I never went to the prom, kissed a girl, or held a woman's hand until my sophomore year in college. When my classmates were out "cruising for chicks" in their sports cars, I was in my yard playing with trucks.

You're probably thinking, "But Lou, you were a college and professional football coach. You must have been an outstanding player." Actually, I was a mediocre athlete who couldn't start on his high school football team until the latter half of my senior year. When I did play, I was usually the smallest guy on the field. Before every game, I tried to negotiate nonaggression pacts with the opposition in which I promised not to hit them as long as they swore not to hit me. Didn't have much luck there. Most of our opponents were built like condominiums. They took one look at my frail form and immediately recognized I had no leverage in this transaction.

Since I wasn't physically gifted, I must have been intellectually blessed, right? Yeah, I was so smart I had to keep my intellect hidden from everyone, lest they be blinded by its brilliance. I graduated in the lower half of my high school class (and my principal later claimed we were a particularly slow-witted group that year). College? That was for the scholars who finished ahead of me. Once I received my diploma, all I wanted out of life was a steel mill job, $5 in my pocket, a girlfriend, and a 1949 Chevrolet.

Nothing wrong with those things, but I was dreaming small.

Wade Watts, my high school football coach, expanded my vista. He suggested to my parents that I go to college with an eye toward becoming a coach. As far as I was concerned, he may as well have suggested I swim to Mars. No one in my family on either side had ever gone beyond high school. We were relatively poor—I was born during the Great Depression—and college should have been beyond our means. But Coach Watts's words filled my parents with determination. My mother took that job as a nurse's aide; the rest of my family also contributed. All of my relatives—particularly my Uncle Leo, who called me champ and constantly told me how special I was—encouraged me to excel in academia. How could I fail with so many good people behind me.

So I became the first Holtz to go to college. Today, I can't imagine where I would be without that education. I've done things I never should have dreamed of as a young man. Except I did dream of them. And that's the point.

Of course, any dream is mere idleness unless you act on it. It takes hard work and dedication to make your dreams real. You must also turn a deaf ear toward those naysayers. Never listen to anyone who tells you your dream is impossible. The next time someone tries to discourage your aspiration, take a close look at him. I'll wager that person hasn't accomplished much in his or her life. Do you think President Clinton would discourage a young person from a divorced home located in a small town in a small state from dreaming of becoming our nation's chief executive?

Any genuinely successful person will tell you to ignore the odds when they are stacked against you and go for it.

Surround yourself with encouragers. Sometimes you need another positive perspective to recognize the limits you place on yourself. I just heard of a fellow who had been thinking about taking up the saxophone. He had loved music all his life and had long harbored a yearning to play with a professional jazz band. However, just as he was ready to purchase an instrument and begin lessons, he backed off. When his wife asked him why he was hesitating, the gentleman replied, "I'm forty-five. I just realized it will take five years of intense practice before I'm ready to play in public. I'll be fifty by then." His wife put him straight by asking, "And how old will you be in five years if you don't study the saxophone?" It took him all of thirty seconds to get that message. He bought the sax. Four years later, he is gigging every weekend in local jazz clubs.

The Gold Cadillac

A salesman was not enjoying much success, largely because he lacked motivation. One day, he passed his local car dealer and saw a gold Cadillac in the showroom. Sticker price: $33,000. The salesman didn't have that kind of money, but he wanted that car. He sat behind the wheel to better visualize what it would be like to own one. When he went home, he decorated the walls with pictures of the gold Cadillac. He did the same at this office. He even pasted photos of the car on the dashboard of his old jalopy.

Inspired by his goal, this man became a crackerjack sales-man. Every time he made a sale, he put $100 in a box under his bed. For every $1,000 he accumulated, he made one trip to the showroom to sit behind that Caddy's steering wheel.

All the Cadillac salespeople thought he was nuts. They were certain he would never save enough money to purchase that car. Less than six months after he first visited the Cadillac showroom, the gentleman walked in and counted out $33,000 in cash. He drove off with the car, leaving behind a pack of stunned salespeople. You can attain your dreams by keeping them in front of you. Nothing is impossible if you prioritize. (A lesson this fellow's wife learned. After she saw the car, she did some dreaming of her own. The salesman woke up the next morning and went into the bathroom to shave, only to find pic-tures of a diamond ring and fur coat pasted to the mirror.)

I Find a Little Bit of Magic

A turning point in my life occurred in 1966, when I went to the University of South Carolina as a defensive coach under Marvin Bass. My wife, Beth, was eight months pregnant with our third child, Kevin, and we had spent every penny we had in the bank for a down payment on a home. We were in the middle of spring practice when I woke up one Monday morn-ing to this headline: "Marvin Bass Resigns." I immediately said to my wife, "I wonder if he is related to my head coach." Of course, by the time I was halfway through the story's first paragraph, I knew the subject of the headline was my head coach.

I was flabbergasted. We had no idea Coach Bass was even contemplating resignation. According to the report, he had accepted a position as head coach in the Canadian Football League. That afternoon, the assistant coaches met with our university's president, Thomas F. Jones. He told us he was determined to hire the best coach available. President Jones further warned us that whomever that person was, he might very well prefer to bring in his own staff as a condition of his employment. We immediately understood that our jobs were in jeopardy.

After an extensive search, President Jones hired Paul Dietzel. An understandable choice. Paul had been an outstanding coach with West Point; he had also coached LSU to a National Championship. Coach Dietzel and I didn't know each other. Which was not good news for me. Like most head coaches, he wanted his staff to be composed largely of people he had worked with previously. Paul retained only two of Coach Bass's assistant coaches. I wasn't one of them.

I was unemployed for over a month, a long time for someone like me. Our savings account was down to four figures—about $10.95. With a growing family to support, I was feeling pressure. It would have been an unbearable period if not for my wife. She could not have been more supportive or encouraging. Beth never complained. She went to work as an X-ray technician to help keep us in groceries. She also bought me the motivational book I referred to earlier, David Schwartz's *The Magic of Thinking Big*. In his chapter on goals, David wrote that anyone who was bored by life had probably forgotten his or her dreams. He invited readers to get back in touch with them. As a first step, we were to list all the things we had ever wanted to accomplish. I had a lot of time on my hands, so I took out a pencil and paper and divided my list into five categories of things I wanted to accomplish:

1.   As a husband/father

2.   Spiritually

3.   Professionally

4.   Financially

5.   Simply for excitement

It was with the fifth category that I let my imagination run wild. Here are some of the things I included:

1.   Jump out of an airplane.

2.   Land a jet fighter on an aircraft carrier.

3.   Travel the ocean in a submarine.

4.   Go white-water rafting on the Snake River at Hell's Canyon.

5.   Be on *The Tonight Show starring Johnny Carson.*

6.   Attend a White House dinner with the president.

7.   Meet the pope.

8.   Go on an African Safari.

9.   Become a scratch golfer and play the Top 50 golf courses in the world.

10.   Run with the bulls in Pamplona (provided I was matched with a much slower person).

And on it went. I had 107 goals on my original list. When I told my wife I was determined that we do all of them, she said, "Gee that's great, honey, but why don't you add 'I want to find a job.'" Good note—the list expanded to 108. We've managed to achieve 99 of those dreams—including dining at the White House and meeting the Pope. We are still working on the others. From the moment I made that list, we became participants rather than spectators in our life. You do the same, and you'll find you won't want to spend too much time sleeping; you'll be afraid you might miss something.

On the Wings of a Dream

A few years back, I traveled to Paw Paw, Michigan, to take skydiving lessons. For my first jump, our pilots took their plane 10,000 feet into the air. I free-fell through those first 5,000 feet in forty-five seconds, pulled the chute, and fell the rest of the way in seven and a half minutes. Hovering 5,000 feet above the earth is an awe-inspiring experience. I'll never forget the excitement I felt when they first opened up the door. The plane's motor was roaring, the wind was blowing through me. Against that glorious backdrop of pure sky, you lose all sense of time, motion, and space. Though you plummet through the atmosphere, you are transcendent, humbled yet exhilarated. You are no longer a merger of ego and id, you are pure consciousness, in and of the moment. You are the moment!

And there is no way I'm ever doing that sucker again!

Every time I'm in an airplane, I reflect on my leap through the universe. It's something I'll never forget. I'll also never forget—or forgive—the two guys who pushed me out the door after I told them I had changed my mind. Hey, they did me a favor. When you add a little risk to your life, you bolster your courage. You also begin to believe that all things are possible.

How to Succeed in Show Business By Really Trying

There's nothing wrong with being frivolous with some of the dreams on your list. That helps make this exercise fun. For years, I wanted to appear on *The Tonight Show starring Johnny Carson*. I would have done it too, except no ever invited me. So I mounted a one-man campaign designed to get me on that show. Whenever I appeared anywhere as a guest speaker, I always did some magic trick. When I was finished, I would ask the audience, "How many of you would like to see me do that trick on the Johnny Carson show?" After the audience applauded—boy were they a polite bunch—I would say, "That's great. If you would write to Johnny Carson and tell him you would like me to be on his show, I would be forever grateful."

I did this for several years without any results. However, in 1977 my Arkansas team was scheduled to play Oklahoma in the Orange Bowl. NBC—which carried the Carson show nationally—was going to televise the game. A few days before the contest, the opposing coach and I spoke at a luncheon. I told some jokes, did another magic trick, and made my usual pitch for a spot on Johnny's program.

At the luncheon's conclusion, a gentleman approached me and said, "I'm Merle Schlosser. I'm the president of NBC, and I want you to be on *The Tonight Show*." I was shocked. Of course, I wanted to do the show. Don't put any dream on your list unless you intend to fulfill it. But in all fairness, I had to warn Mr. Schlosser that none of the experts thought my team had a chance to win the Orange Bowl. Arkansas was, after all, a 24-point underdog. Mr. Schlosser said, "I don't care about that, you're coming on. And not as any one o'clock guest either, you're eleven forty-five material." Going on at 11:45 meant I would be the first guest to appear after Johnny's monologue. It was the most coveted spot on the show! What could top that?

How about proving the prognosticators wrong by shellacking Oklahoma 31–6 in the Orange Bowl?

That's exactly what we did. Nine months later, I was on Johnny's show. Winning coach in the Orange Bowl to *Tonight Show* guest, all in a year. Can you understand why I am convinced that your dreams can never be too big?

Tackling the Big Chief

Five years ago, I took my wife, mother-in-law, four children, and their spouses white-water rafting on the Snake River in Hell's Canyon. We planned to be on the river for four days and three nights. I had no idea how perilous this adventure could be. It looked like fun. However, two people drowned in the river just before we arrived; apparently, the rapids were particularly treacherous during that time of the year.

We hired professional guides to accompany us. Clad in my life jacket, I had just gotten into our raft when one of the guides announced that we'd better be prepared for a turbulent excursion. He was going to take us through the "Big Chief," a bona fide Class 5 rapid. This was a stretch of waterway only Freddy Krueger could love. For those of you who have never rafted, a Class 5 is the second most dangerous rapid you can challenge. Only a Class 6 poses greater potential jeopardy. What is a Class 6? Niagara Falls. Not the current leading to the Falls, but the Falls themselves.

As soon as we hit the Big Chief, the Big Chief hit back. A wave tumbled me heels over head out of the raft and into the water. Though I didn't realize it at the time, my thumb was broken in four places. It's amazing how you don't notice a little thing like a broken finger when you are drowning.

I was stuck under the raft. No one had taught me to hand-walk along its underside, the proper way to escape from such a predicament. So what did I do? Friends, Lou Holtz is not one to remain calm when a situation calls for panic. I couldn't think of anything, not with my life passing before my eyes in glorious Technicolor. So I let myself sink. Logic told me that if I dropped straight down, the raft would pass overhead. Then I could swim back up to an open space, and signal my friends for help.

Unfortunately, rapids don't know from logic. When I bobbed back to the surface, I was still under the raft. Now I was genuinely frightened (I had just been faking it before). I've always been able to focus myself by thinking of the acronym WIN, which stands for What's Important Now. Well, that was a no-brainer. What was important was for me to get out from under that raft! Once I concentrated on that objective, I figured out for myself how to hand-walk from under the raft.

That did the trick. As the raft drifted free, I was able to pull my head above the water. If I hadn't focused on what needed to be done and then taken the steps required to obtain that objective, I would have ended up as lunch for a school of salmon. I think everyone should use WIN as a motivational tool. If you continually ask yourself "What's Important Now?" you won't waste time on the trivial. This is the second best piece of advice anyone can give you.

What's the first? Stay out of white-water rafts.

Keep Your Eyes on the Ball: Think Win!

In 1984, I stunned many college football fans and writers when I agreed to become head coach of the University of Minnesota. Heck, I even stunned myself. I thought I would spend the rest of my life at the University of Arkansas. During my seven years with Arkansas, my teams had compiled the best win-loss record in the university's history, as well as the second-best win-loss record in the history of the Southwest Conference.

Despite our gaudy stats, the university terminated me. This action came without warning. I had spent most of a Saturday morning interviewing John Gutikunst for the position of defensive coordinator. He accepted the next morning, and I was excited about our prospects for the upcoming season. That very afternoon, our athletic director Frank Broyles and his assistant Lou Farrell gave me the grim news.

I respected Frank Broyles. I'm sure he had his reasons for dismissing me, but to this day I have no idea what they were. When they told me of their decision, I asked if there was anything I could do to change their minds. Frank said no.

I returned home devastated. My wife was in a state of shock. Within two hours, news of my dismissal was on national television. Well, at least a version of the news was on TV. Some broadcasters interrupted their call of an NFL game to announce that Lou Holtz had resigned as Arkansas's head football coach.

Fifteen minutes later, Harvey Mackay—a friend of Paul Giel, the athletic director at the University of Minnesota—phoned to invite me to Minnesota to discuss the head coaching position. I was already aware that Minnesota was desperate to find an experienced coach. Its selection committee had already contacted five prospects; all five had rejected their offers. With good reason. Palermo had not been conquered as often as Minnesota's football team. As I mentioned earlier, it had suffered 17 consecutive defeats, most of them by wide margins.

As I've already mentioned, I had been one of the original five candidates who rejected the job. At the time I turned it down, I was head coach of one of the most successful teams in the country. We played in a hospitable climate. I did not want to relocate to Minnesota. I had met only three people from that state, but each of them had blond hair and blue ears. Brrrr! No thank you. However, now I was out of work. Twenty degrees below zero suddenly seemed almost tropical to me. I was also in a mood to prove something, to tackle the biggest challenge I could find. Minnesota was certainly all of that. So I accepted the job with one condition.

From the time I had entered college football, I had one objective: to become head coach at Notre Dame. I was candid about my desire with the University of Minnesota's administrators. They weren't happy about it and I didn't blame them. What employer wants to hear that the person they are about to hire has his heart set on working somewhere else?

Notre Dame was not a pipe dream for me. The university's new athletic director, Gene Corrigan, had tried to hire me on three different occasions when he was with the University of Virginia. So I thought I had a decent chance to become his head coach at Notre Dame if the position ever opened again. Knowing that, I wasn't about to sign any contract that prevented me from accepting Gene's offer if it came.

Had Minnesota not been desperate for a coach, they probably would have told me to mosey on down the road. Instead, we reached a compromise which became known as "The Notre Dame Clause." The two governing sections of that clause stated I could accept the head coaching job in South Bend provided:

1.   Notre Dame contacted me about the position. I could not make the first call.

2.   The University of Minnesota had to earn a Bowl bid before I would be free to leave.

This seemed more than fair. It took care of my needs while guaranteeing that the university would not have to endure another long search for a coach if I left. I was confident that if

I could turn around Minnesota's football team, Corrigan would call me as soon as the Notre Dame job became available. If we were successful enough to earn a Bowl bid, Minnesota would have no difficulty finding my replacement. Coaches would be fighting each other to win what would then be an attractive position.

As I've written in a previous chapter, coaching at the University of Minnesota was a marvelous experience. During my time there, I often consulted with Harvey Mackay, another visionary who knows how to get things done. Both of us dreamed of getting a modern practice field for our football team. Within eight months, we had one that we both helped design.

Our next objective was to attract more fans to our games. The continual losing had repelled all but our most die-hard followers. We appealed to the pride of everyone in the Minneapolis–St. Paul area by naming our defensive team "St. Paul" and the offensive squad "Minneapolis." Then we asked the citizens of both cities to come out in support of their team. They responded enthusiastically. We drew over 40,000 fans for our first spring game. After we showed how competitive we could be on the field during my first year, we sold out the stadium for every date the following season.

We played many exciting games during that second year. Against Barry Switzer's University of Oklahoma squad, we were behind by 6 points with less than two minutes left in the game. We had a first-and-10 with the ball inside Oklahoma's 15 yard line. Unfortunately, we didn't convert the touchdown and lost by 6. No disgrace. Oklahoma went on to win the National Championship that season.

We played Purdue only one week after they had beaten Notre Dame, 35–14. At halftime we led Purdue and Jim Everett, their All-Star quarterback, 35–3. We went on to win that game in what was hailed as the biggest upset of the season.

The winning continued. At the end of the year, Minnesota accepted a bid to play Clemson in the Independence Bowl. Three days later, Notre Dame announced that Gerry Faust had resigned. They contacted me shortly after. I was in a position to accept their offer because I had applied my "WIN" philosophy during my contract negotiations with the University of Minnesota. My long-term and short-term goals were in conflict. They had to be resolved. So I asked myself, "What's important now?" got the answer, and insisted on my Notre Dame clause. Whenever you face a crucial decision, think WIN!

Scoring a WIN At NC State

Before I joined North Carolina State as its head coach, the team had averaged only 23,000 fans per game. Only 22,500 attended the first NC State game I coached. There are few things more forlorn looking than a half-empty football stadium. Our stands could seat more than 41,000, and it discouraged our players that we weren't coming close to capacity. The team just had to draw more fans.

We devised a guerrilla marketing campaign built around widely distributed pamphlets that extolled the value of NC State football. Our pamphlet pointed out that the average father spent less than an hour a week participating in some activity with his children. Bringing them to one of our football games would triple that quality time. We asked parents to come and cheer on their team while visualizing the day their children would attend NC State as students. Our objective was to make these families part of our family.

It was a successful promotion. Attendance jumped to 39,000 by our second contest. It would be the last time we played before a single empty seat. During my remaining four years with the school, we averaged approximately 45,000 fans per game. Yes, we exceeded our capacity. We were able to do this by letting students sit on blankets on a large grass hill located behind the end zone. I am not sure how many of them actually watched the game, but they seemed to thoroughly enjoy themselves.

And why not? We certainly gave them something to see. Our team was invited to four consecutive Bowl games. I take no credit for that. It really didn't matter who coached those teams. I knew when I accepted the job that they were going to win. There were too many good athletes on that roster. And every one of them was dedicated to the same objective. Our players got up each morning knowing what was important to them that day. I didn't have to motivate them. They stoked themselves on their own. Building a successful team is easy. Just bring together a group of people who dream of doing the impossible and have them follow the WIN formula. It worked at NC State and at every other school where I have coached.

We Get What We Expect

I find that we get out of life exactly what we expect of it. This became clear to me during my tenure as head coach at the College of William and Mary. When I first accepted the position, I reviewed our schedule. It was not a cheering document. We were going to have to compete against such juggernauts as the University of North Carolina and Wake Forest—cochampions of the ACC the previous season—the University of West Virginia, Virginia Tech, Tulane, Miami of Florida, and other teams of comparable ability. I didn't care much for our chances, didn't think we would even be competitive.

I was right.

Our opponents beat us decisively week after week. Most of the blame for our poor record rested with me. I had never been a head coach before; I made many mistakes while I was learning on the job. As an assistant coach, I had made suggestions, but never had to shoulder the ultimate responsibility for choosing a strategy. When you are a head coach, all final decisions belong to you. And you often have to make them on the spot in front of 40,000 to 50,000 screaming critics. That's pressure.

By my second year, I honestly felt that we could compete with the powerhouse teams, but I doubted we could beat them. Again, we lived up—or down—to my expectations. We never lost a game by more than 6 points, but lose we did. North Carolina beat us 36–35 when its team nailed a two-point conversion in the game's last minute. Wake Forest bested us 33–28 when its quarterback scored on an option play in the last minute of that contest. We also lost to Virginia Tech when Don Strock threw a touchdown pass in, yep, the last minute of the game to beat us by 3. West Virginia scored a 27–24 victory when they ran back a punt late in the game. We did beat Tulane University, which was undefeated at the time, and we won most of our other games.

You could see we had the talent to play tough against anyone. But confidence was the difference between us and the more elite teams. We played them expecting to lose, so we did. I learned a valuable lesson that season: Always expect the best for yourself, then you won't be surprised when you get it.

Woody Always Believed

When I joined Woody Hayes as an assistant coach at Ohio State in 1968, our prospects were poor. The team had been mediocre in 1967 and Coach Hayes was under immense pressure to reverse its fortunes. It wouldn't be easy. We were going to start sixteen sophomores that year. Since freshmen were ineligible to play back then, this would be their first year of college competition. Had I known how untested our team would be, I might not have accepted Woody's offer. I thought we would be fortunate to play .500 ball.

Coach Hayes did not share my concerns. When he talked to his staff during a summer meeting, he declared we were heading for the Rose Bowl that season. I thought the only way we were going to the Rose Bowl was if we bought tickets. But at least one of his assistants was already a true believer. When Coach Hayes finished speaking, Lou McCullough pointed out that the Rose Bowl would be held in California on January 1, 1969. That meant we could go to Las Vegas for five days before returning to L.A. for the coaches convention on January 6. So we asked Coach Hayes if he would send us to Vegas, all expenses paid, as our reward for winning the National Championship. (And, oh yes, we got our trip to Vegas!)

It was all a big joke at first. However, we mentioned it after every win. Which meant we talked about it every week, because no one could beat us. The more we won, the more we started to believe that we were Vegas bound. We kept right on believing until we reached the Rose Bowl. Our opponents were a formidable Southern Cal team lead by a brilliant running back named O.J. Simpson.

Woody was convinced that if we could stop Simpson, we would paralyze USC's offense. Coach wanted me to coordinate a strategy designed to contain O.J. I had several ideas how to accomplish this; Coach didn't like any of them. We argued over ways and means for several days without coming to a resolution. Finally, he said to me, "I don't care how you stop him, just do it. He better not score a single touchdown."

There was something ominous in the way he said that. I knew right then that if O.J. scored, I was going to feel the Wrath of Hayes.

O.J. didn't get so much as a whiff of end zone during the first quarter. Our defense rendered him a non-factor. But in the second quarter, with USC at first-and-10 on their own 20 yard line, the Juice ripped off an 80-yard run for a touchdown. So much for containment. I was in the press box when he made the drive and didn't see Coach Hayes until we were in the locker room for halftime.

You might say he was upset. Coach grabbed me by my windpipe with his left hand and hoisted me off the floor. Don't get the wrong idea. Coach wasn't trying to hurt me. This was merely his way of making sure he had my undivided attention. As he throttled me, he screamed at the top of his lungs, "Why did O.J. run 80 yards against our defense?" All I could say was, "I don't know, Coach. I guess that was all he needed." Coach released his grip and warned me that O.J. had better not score again in the second half.

We kept him off the scoreboard the rest of the game, but it wasn't easy. It was obvious we didn't have a player of his equal on our roster. Didn't matter. We beat USC 27–16 to finish the year undefeated. I am convinced that we won our surprising National Championship because Coach Hayes dreamed it and then persuaded everyone else on our club to buy into his dream.

Dreamers All

Dreamers move the world. My friend Richard Heckman, whom I've mentioned previously, took over U.S. Filter when it was a floundering company doing only $17 million in business. He dreamed of building it into the world's largest water filtration and treatment company. Seven years later, it could claim over $2.5 billion in annual sales. Mike Harper, of ConAgra, asked me to speak before his employees in 1980 when I was at the University of Arkansas. It was a $700 million company when I went to its headquarters in Omaha, Nebraska. Most people would be satisfied with that impressive number, but Mike was always envisioning ways to expand his business. By the time he retired, ConAgra was doing over $25 billion in worldwide business. Think of the many jobs these two men have created, the lives they've improved, simply because they refused to accept the status quo. They followed their imaginations to bigger things and everyone associated with them benefited.

Good things happen when you act on your dreams. Another friend, Glen McCusker, never graduated college, but that didn't mean he was going to accept a second-rate life. He saw a business opportunity—a computer software company—he believed in and borrowed $50,000 in start-up capital from his parents. Their faith in their son's dream was so strong, they raised the funds by mortgaging their home. Today, Glen is the CEO of Viking Components, a $300 million business. Dreamers don't fantasize, they make things happen. They not only have immense confidence in themselves, they have it in others. They never undervalue the talents of those they lead.

Every one of us will encounter a number of potentially lucrative opportunities in our lifetimes. But opportunity is never a polite thing. It won't stand around waiting for you while you sit trying to decide whether or not to embrace it. You must have the courage to grab it with both hands when it's in front of you. I have been fortunate to speak before nearly every company in the Fortune 500. They all have one thing in common: leaders who dream of greatness all the time. They don't wait for anything. These men and women set lofty goals for themselves and their companies and then surpass them. We can all profit if we follow their examples.

My Friend, Harvey Mackay

To have at least one close friend, someone other than your wife or children that you can always rely on, is a blessing. I've had three in my life and couldn't be more grateful for such abundance. My Uncle Lou Tychonievich was my best friend for fifty years. I could speak with him about anything. He died this past year, and I miss him sorely.

Dick Rosenthal and Harvey Mackay are two more men I can count on. Harvey is like my brother. Not a week goes by that we don't talk at least once. I don't care how depressed you might feel, when Harvey is around you are going to immediately perk up. He is a walking advertisement for the power of positive thinking. Harvey is a successful businessman, father, husband, author, and speaker. You'll never meet a better problem solver. I can't tell you how often I've said to him, "No one has been able to solve this problem, and I'm not sure you can, but I'd like you to try. You're my last resort." Of course, Harvey always comes through. He'll move heaven and earth to help a friend.

Headlines Don't Make Heroes

Some of the greatest achievers win little fame, but they enhance the lives of all they touch. Frank "Digger" Dawson is one of these people. He started a scholarship program for students in my hometown of East Liverpool, Ohio. Digger is always dreaming about how he can raise more money to grow that fund. Hundreds of students have benefited from his generosity. The city should honor him because he is special, but I think we take his good deeds for granted. So I want to take a moment here to honor Digger and everyone like him, people who help others with no expectation of reward or recognition. Tell me your definition of a genuine hero, because I just gave you mine.

Wasted Talent

In the movie *A Bronx Tale*, a father, played by Robert DeNiro, tells his son, "The saddest thing in the world is wasted talent." How true. I have seen people blessed with preternatural ability who never made first team or even second string because they didn't dream big enough. For example, a young man we will call Bill Gorch was one of the finest high school basketball players I have ever seen. He lived only ten miles from my hometown and attended Wellsville High. At 6'9", Bill had a nice soft touch on his jump shot and excellent athletic skills. He was a scoring machine. I thought he was comparable or perhaps even better than Jerry Lucas, the great forward who eventually made All-American at Ohio State, helped that school win a National Championship, earned All-Star honors in the National Basketball Association, and played a vital role on a New York Knicks NBA championship team.

When Bill was in his senior year, the mailman was bringing him a mountain of college offers nearly every week. All the big schools wanted to grant him a full athletic scholarship. However, his high school coach had accepted a job with a college in western Ohio. Bill had a good relationship with this coach, so he joined him at this relatively small university.

Bill averaged nearly 50 points a game during his two years of college ball. He scored over 100 points in one contest. Led by this scoring dervish, his team upset many good clubs.

However, the school lacked the money and finances to consistently compete with the big-time college basketball programs. So Bill rarely got the publicity his performances would have attracted had he played at a high-profile university.

After his second year, he dropped out of college. This deprived him of a showcase for NBA scouts. He instead chose to tour with the Harlem Globetrotters as a member of its perennial opponents, the Washington Generals. The Generals are rarely more than just foils for the Globetrotters' on-court antics. Pro scouts think of them primarily as entertainers rather than serious athletes. By joining them, Bill effectively shut the door on an NBA career. That was a shame. I believe he could have been one of the greatest basketball players of all time. The only thing that stopped him from achieving NBA fame was the limitations he placed on himself. He should have dreamed larger.

Turning a Little Into a Lot

I've seen so many athletes who never realized their potential. Throughout my college career, my staff and I have recruited some great high school kicking prospects who were disappointing college players. They cost us victories by missing extra points or easy field goals. On the other hand, when Notre Dame won the National Championship, our kicker was Ted Gradle, a non-scholarship senior who had never before kicked in a game. His successor was 5'4", 120-pound Reggie Ho from Hawaii. You couldn't find two more unlikely candidates for gridiron success. You would have thought both were crazy for even auditioning for our team.

However, neither athlete tried to live up to anyone's expectations but their own. Ted and Reggie both dreamed of becoming outstanding players. They became two of the most productive kickers I have coached. They weren't the most skilled kickers we ever had on our roster, but they got the most out of what they had. Their examples teach us that it is not enough to have talent. Do you have a talent for using your talent? If you don't, you must develop it or you will go through life frustrated. What I love about both men I just mentioned is that they approach life the way they approached football. Today, they are known as Dr. Gradle and Dr. Ho. They've achieved exactly what they wanted because of their power to dream.

Follow the Music Inside You

When I first arrive on a campus to accept a new challenge, I sit down with each of my players and get to know them. I want to discover as much as I can about the player's background. More importantly I want to find out what his aspirations are. One day, a defensive lineman named Dan Hampton walked into my office at the University of Arkansas for one of these chats. Dan was a second-teamer. The moment I saw him I wondered why he wasn't starting. Dan was 6'5", 235 pounds and possessed a natural, athletic grace. He looked like he should be first team. As we spoke, I was also impressed with his obvious intelligence. So what was missing?

When I asked Dan what his goals were, he didn't talk much about football. Instead, he mentioned how he loved music, and wanted to participate in the college band. I suggested he hit the weight room. Not because it would make him a stronger player—although the thought had occurred to me—but because it would enable him to play piano in the school marching band. It takes a lot of power to lug the marching piano; there weren't many people who possessed the necessary strength and stamina.

Once we tapped into his dream, Dan rededicated himself to his training. He found time for his music while becoming an All American with us and a star defensive lineman with the Chicago Bears. I believe he will eventually be inducted into the Hall of Fame. Dan is an example of someone who used one dream to attain another.

By the way, I want to take time to publicly apologize to Dan. I didn't know it back then but one of his other dreams was to play in the Hula Bowl, our college All-Star game. I could've selected him for that squad one year, but took Jimmy Walker, another Arkansas defensive lineman instead. At the time, I reasoned that Jimmy was only 5'11" and 225 pounds. He was a great college player, but I doubted he had the size to compete in the pros. I figured Dan would have an outstanding NFL and would get to Hawaii when he played in the Pro Bowl (the NFL's all-star game). Dan proved me an excellent prognosticator. He did make All-Pro. However, I did him a disservice by not picking him for Hawaii when I had the chance. Notice, though, that he eventually got there on his own. Dreamers never quit.

Now start visualizing some dreams of your own. Compile an extensive list. Write down everything you hope to achieve in life. Break the list down into five categories as I did. Unrein your imagination with this exercise. Have fun with this! If you see yourself as the President of the United States or the Emperor of Borneo, write it down. Then make sure you do something every day to realize one of your dreams. You are going to encounter adversity; nothing worth having ever comes easy. But you will also find yourself waking up hungry to take big, satisfying bites out of life. That's what I call the breakfast of champions.

7

YOU ARE WHAT YOU THINK: NURTURING YOUR SELF-IMAGE

Just before embarking for Kent State University to start my college education, I overheard a conversation in the local grocery store. Two women in the aisle next to mine—they had no idea I was on the other side of the cereal and English muffins— were chattering away. I'm not an eavesdropper and normally wouldn't have paid any attention to their conversation. Except one of them mentioned my name. "Isn't it a shame," she said, "that the Holtz's are wasting what little money they have sending Lou to college."

I didn't need to hear that, but I couldn't fault her logic. After all, Kent State had a demanding curriculum, one that could challenge even honor students. I had graduated in the lower half of my high school class. Who would confuse me for university material? My mother and family were the only people in town who believed in me. Even Mr. Dawson, the dean of boys at my high school, discouraged my academic aspirations. He suggested I take a job at the steel mill or the pottery plant.

These negative assessments of my ability discouraged but did not defeat me. Instead, they motivated me. When people have no faith in you, you can respond in one of two ways: You can accept their opinions as fact and live whatever small life they have selected for you. Or you can dedicate yourself to proving them wrong. I chose the latter. You've never seen anyone prouder than my parents and I were the day I accepted my college diploma. What a boost to my self-esteem!

I've always encouraged our college players to go for the sheepskin. A college degree does not prove that you are more intelligent or gifted than someone who doesn't possess one. A diploma is a testament to your discipline, perseverance, and comprehension skills. It says you are willing to pay a price to excel. It cannot impart happiness or success; you must find those things on your own. But it should give you a sense of pride in accomplishment.

Builder or Basher: Which Are You?

Terry Ewert, an executive producer with CBS Sports, once told me that everybody falls into one of three categories: Those who can count and those who can't. You want to read that again? After much observation, I have concluded he was wrong. We should instead divide individuals into two categories: Those who lift you up and those who pull you down. We've all seen spouses who support each other and couples who treat bickering like an Olympic event. When they're not actively engaged in it, they are off somewhere practicing. Some parents nurture their child's self-image, others provoke their child's self-loathing. And don't we all know people who never open their mouths unless it is to deprecate something?

Feel sorry for those poor souls. They tear down only to build themselves up. We must teach them by example that the greatest responsibility each of us has is to raise the life condition of everyone we touch. Remember: Encouragement builds success; discouragement breeds contempt. No one can deny the law of cause and effect. Your friends and associates will not think well of you unless you think well of yourself. You cannot think well of yourself unless you think well of others.

Most negativists are envious because they lack confidence. That's an observation made from personal experience. The author of this book was once one of the most insecure men you could ever meet. I maligned others hoping that I would look better by comparison. I was degrading myself and bringing misery to those around me.

My insecurity occasionally manifested itself as spousal jealousy. In thirty-seven years, my wife has never given me legitimate cause to turn green-eyed, but that didn't stop me from going into a funk whenever another male paid her any attention. If I saw her in conversation with some man at a cocktail party, the tapes in my head would zoom into overdrive. I would tell myself that this fellow was handsomer, smarter, and better built than I. Then I asked myself why she wouldn't rather be with him than me.

No one would find much comfort in the answers I received. After speaking to this paragon of maleness, Beth would regret our marriage, I was certain. How could I possibly compete with this or any other man? My self-flagellation would continue along these lines for the rest of the evening. Then, not content with beating up myself, I'd turn on her.

I would unfairly criticize my wife's every fault throughout our car ride home. As there weren't many to harp on, I'd invent a few. My objective was to make her feel lucky to have someone like me, given all her shortcomings. This is embarrassing to write. What I did was inexcusable. I cannot apologize enough for the grief I caused that fine woman. Believe it or not, she's still with me. It turned out she loved me more than I did. And now I realize, I'm the lucky one.

More Than Meets the Eye

So much of our self-image is linked to our appearance. I find that most people don't much care for the faces that greet them in the mirror every morning. I'm no different. For example, in 1988 Notre Dame started the season 10–0 and was ranked number one in the country. In one of the biggest games of the year, we beat unbeaten, second-ranked USC, 27–10.

After the game I was floating. Our team stayed overnight in California. We rose the next morning to attend a Notre Dame mass and prayer breakfast. Then we took the team to Disneyland. When we first entered the main park, press photographers from various publications asked me if they could snap our captain's picture with Mickey Mouse and Donald Duck. After he complied, they asked me to pose. However, I didn't draw Mickey and Donald as partners. Oh no. They stuck me in between Pluto and Goofy. I thought that was unusual, but I didn't say anything. Before anyone snapped a shutter, I pulled my Notre Dame hat down around my eyes. I was hoping no one would be able to recognize me.

That picture appeared in the *L.A. Times* shortly after we returned to South Bend. The first sentence of the caption under it read, "Here is Lou Holtz, head football coach of Notre Dame's Fighting Irish, at Disneyland with Pluto and Goofy." Then the next sentence read, in big bold letters, **"LOU HOLTZ IS THE ONE IN THE MIDDLE."**

Talk about your boosts to the old ego.

I get those all time. If I am walking through an airport, someone will come up behind me and say, "Hey, Coach. Everybody says we look alike." I immediately get excited. Why not? It's not every day you get to meet Mel Gibson or Robert Redford. When I turn around to greet this hunk, I invariably think, "Oh no, I can't possibly look like that!" One time a man approached me and said, "Has anyone ever told you that you look a lot like that Lou Holtz fellow, the football coach?" I smiled and said, "Yes, it happens to me constantly." He laughed and said, "It kind of makes you mad, doesn't it?"

These comments hurt, because my appearance disappointed me. I have since discovered that I'm not alone. Most people don't admire their looks. Why do you think cosmetic surgeons do such a booming business today? We all know men and women who agonize over every physical imperfection. And no matter how many cuts and tucks they subject themselves to, they are never going to be happy. Doctors can remove the blemishes and wrinkles on their skin, but not the ones on their souls. Hairpieces and weaves can disguise a bald spot, but not your insecurity.

Don't obsess on your appearance. Have you ever noticed how an otherwise ordinary looking person can command a room if he or she glows with esteem? Genuine beauty comes from within. Once I learned that, I changed my focus. I learned to take pride in who I was and what I accomplished rather than how I combed my hair.

Cultivate your self-confidence. The more you believe in yourself, the better you'll handle adversity. Never underestimate your assets; never overestimate another person's pluses. In fact, don't compare yourself to anyone. You are singular. There is no one else like you in the world. What could be more beautiful or compelling than something so rare?

We're in This Thing Together

Our world is a vast laboratory. It is a place where we can observe behavior—our own as well as others'. I am continually amazed how some people can be so relentlessly positive, while others can never see the upside of anything. Why do some individuals greet hardship with hope, while others run from success? Oscar Wilde once said, "It is not enough that I succeed, my friends must also fail." Brother, was he insecure. Too many people act as they believe wrecking their neighbors' furniture will make theirs look better by comparison. It doesn't work that way. Root for everyone to succeed. The great New Orleans blues singer Aaron Neville performs solo and as a member of the Neville Brothers. When Aaron received his first gold record, he said, "I'm glad for this honor, but I won't be completely happy until my brothers earn a gold record, too." That's an attitude we all should share.

Even the Great Ones Doubt

As a coach, I found that all the great players I ever recruited held two concomitant opinions of themselves. They all wanted to compete with the best. And they all questioned their ability to play on that level. I empathized with this; I had many of those same feelings myself. I would say to the recruit, "During a person's lifetime, there are only a couple of opportunities that come your way. If you possess the courage and self-confidence to grasp them, they can change your life." However, many people are too insecure to recognize their own potential. We must find the courage to take advantage of every opportunity life brings us. You can't taste victory without risking defeat. If you stand paralyzed by doubt, someone else will drive into the end zone ahead of you for the touchdown. Remember, a turtle only makes progress if it is willing to stick its neck out.

Give Them a Clear Picture

False confidence, however, can be worse than no confidence. I would never inflate an athlete's ego by making him think he was more talented than he was. Tell a player he's outstanding and he will be demoralized when he discovers he isn't. He'll also never trust you again. However, you can't disparage people's abilities or they will never perform well. Like the old song says, you have to accentuate the positive. But don't hype it. As long as you keep your criticism constructive, you can help people build on their assets by pointing out their liabilities.

Treat your teams the same way. Tell a team it's unbeatable and it will fall apart with its first loss. Then the finger-pointing begins. Teammates start blaming outside factors for their record instead of their own inadequacies. What can you expect? You told them they were great and they believed you. Any defeats they suffer must be someone else's fault. Of course, on that inevitable day when they realize they are not as good as you claimed, that you sold them a bill of goods, you've lost them. They'll never believe you again. Always be upbeat but realistic with your people.

See the Shot Before You Make the Shot

All the great golfers I have known visualize their success before it happens. They never entertain doubts. If they miss a putt, they will always tap down a spike mark, giving you the impression that it is never their fault. You must have the same self-confidence to compete on their level. I don't care what you do, never question your ability. Do everything you can to improve your performance, but when game time comes take the field thinking you are the best.

This Turtle Could Play

When people choose happiness and success, nothing can stop them. Great things are bound to happen. For example, during my early years at Notre Dame, we had a player from Baltimore named Mike Brennan. He come to us as a tight end. Mike was 6'4" and 210 pounds—an average weight for his height—yet he may have been the slowest athlete I have ever coached. Naturally, the players nicknamed him "Turtle." This was very disparaging . . . to turtles. I mean those reptiles were relatively quick compared to Mike. Heck, I've seen corpses that could have spotted him 5 yards and still beat him in a sprint.

After his first season, I doubted he would ever play for us, but I liked having him on the team. He had a wonderful spirit and worked harder than anyone. Mike could have focused on his shortcomings and quit. Who would have blamed him? Instead, he chose to believe in himself. He was always the first one on the practice field and the last to leave. Mike rehearsed all his assignments until he had them down perfectly. His self-confidence, backed by his all-out effort, made all the difference. Mike not only eventually won a starting position with us, he went on to play four seasons as an offensive lineman in the NFL. He provides us with some of our best evidence of the power of positive thinking.

Don't Flinch

In 1987, I drove to Chicago to have lunch with Carl Pohlad. During our meal, Carl said, "Successful people don't flinch."

In the Eye of a Hurricane

Winners exude self-confidence. Watching a football game, you can usually predict early in the contest who is going to win just by observing how each team carries itself. Certain teams set up as if they know they have you beaten before the game even starts. A club like that can destroy an opponent's morale.

When Notre Dame played coach Jimmy Johnson and his University of Miami Hurricanes in 1987, they had an outstanding receiver named Michael Irvin. Every time he made a good play—something he did often—Michael incited the crowd with antics that most of us would call "hot-dogging." You see players do this all the time. They run into the end zone for a TD, then spike the ball while breaking into a flashdance. Some players indulge in this choreography just to call attention to themselves, but for Michael, hot-dogging was a weapon. He used it to challenge and intimidate, to let his opponents know he was going to beat them all afternoon.

Michael and his Miami teammates did top us that day. However, by the following year, our team had developed the attitude that we could vanquish anybody. I'm sure Jimmy and the Hurricanes felt the same way. They came into our 1988 rematch ready to defend the longest regular season winning streak of any college football team in the country.

We held the home field advantage for that game. The night before the contest, I got up to speak at a pep rally in front of 25,000 students. I kept my remarks brief. I asked the fans to do three things for our team. First, I wanted them to cheer louder for Notre Dame at this game than they had ever cheered before. Second, I wanted them to comport themselves with class, as they always did. Third, I wanted them to let Jimmy Johnson and his team know that we were going to beat them like an old yard dog.

By the time I had addressed that throng, it had been so late in the evening, I didn't expect my comments to hit the morning papers. Was I wrong! I woke up the next day to headlines blaring, "Lou Holtz Predicts Victory Over Hurricanes." My first reaction was that I had pulled one of the all-time rock-headed blunders. Miami was awfully good; they didn't need any help from me to get psyched for this game. I could just picture my words being posted throughout their locker room.

Then I thought, "Heck, what difference does it make? The Hurricanes are going to be up to play us no matter what I said." Jimmy Johnson could have given motivation lessons to Dale Carnegie. He was, and still is, an outstanding coach who would have his team completely prepared for any game of this magnitude. The more I thought about those headlines, the less they concerned me.

Besides, I had accomplished exactly what I wanted. My outlandish comments at the pep rally—outlandish because they were so out of character for me—weren't aimed at the fans or even the Miami football team. The Fighting Irish of Notre Dame were my targets. I wanted all of our players to realize how much confidence I had in them. This was not smoke I was blowing. I believed with every fiber of my being that we were going to be victorious.

At first, my players had no idea what I was doing. To be honest, I wasn't completely sure myself. But when we gathered for our team meeting, I explained why I thought we would win the game. I pointed out how our team had vastly improved since last season. No one could dispute that. Then I asked how many members of our offense were going to fumble the ball or throw an interception. No one raised a hand. I asked which member of our defense was going to make an interception or recover a fumble. Quite a few hands went up. We went through a litany of assignments. Every time a player's hand rose, I wrote his name on the blackboard alongside the task he had promised to carry out. An exercise such as this encourages your people to make a visual commitment to winning. By the time this meeting was over, our squad believed it was unbeatable.

Two obdurate football teams took the field the next day. Not a player on either side could spell the word "yield." With the score tied at the end of the first quarter, the two teams exchanged ends of the field. As they passed each other, one of Miami's offensive tackles said to our linebacker, Frank Stamms, "This game is going down to the wire, isn't it?" He knew. Miami went into every game certain it would prevail, but now they were facing a team just as confident. We staged our version of Armageddon throughout the afternoon. It was a brute of a football game and, yes, it did go down to the final second. We beat them by a single point. That was a victory that could have gone either way, because neither team knew how to flinch.

Sometimes You Have to Peer Into That Void

Many people don't know what they can do until some circumstance forces them to dig inside themselves. That brings to mind a great friend of mine, Nevitt Stockdale, who passed away this past year after suffering a heart attack. Nevitt was one of the most talented people I have ever known, a college professor with a Ph.D. in mathematics. More important, he was a beautiful soul with a great sense of humor. We used to swim together in the Ohio River when we were teenagers. One afternoon, someone came up with the brilliant idea that we should swim the river's width.

That was no easy challenge. From our side in East Liverpool, Ohio, to the opposite bank in Chester, West Virginia, was nearly a mile. It was so far that when I removed my glasses, I could barely see the other side. I probably should have begged off, but you know how it is with boys. Who wants to be called a chicken? We made an agreement that the guy who finished last would walk the mile back across the bridge, retrieve our car, and drive back over to pick up the rest of us. Just before our race started, Nevitt took me aside and said, "I'm not going. I can't swim that far. I'll get halfway across the river and start drowning. If I survive, my mom will whip my butt good." I told him, "You can make it, Nevitt, and if you can't, I'll save you." He eyed me warily. "You would do that?" he asked. I gave him my word. Of course, Nevitt didn't realize I had an agenda. It was important to me that Nevitt made this swim. Was I trying to build his character? Heck no! Nevitt was the only one in our crowd whom I was certain I could beat to the other side. If he didn't compete, I was going to be the one who would have to hoof back across the bridge to get the car. I didn't want to take that walk; Nevitt represented an insurance policy.

At the count of three, all of us dived into the water. One-fourth of the way across, I spied Nevitt. He's paddling the water, but he's doing great. Halfway over, Nevitt has switched to the breast stroke and he's slicing through the river currents like an Olympic champion. Johnny Weissmuller never looked so good. When we were three-quarters of the way done, I spotted Nevitt again. He wasn't paddling. He wasn't doing the breast stroke. He was too busy drowning.

The comedian Joe E. Lewis once quipped, "A friend in need . . . is a pest!" That's what Nevitt suddenly became. In between swallowing large gulps of the Ohio, he yelled out my name, a loud reminder of our pact. I immediately understood my obligation. A friend was in danger, and I had promised to come to his aid. So I did what any red-blooded American boy would do.

I pretended not to hear him.

Did you think I was going to be the hero of this reel? To be honest, the swim had exhausted me and I was worried that if I attempted a rescue, we would both drown. True, Nevitt was one of my best friends. But that was only as long as my feet could touch dry land or the river's bottom. Nevitt begged, pleaded, and prayed for assistance, but I kept swimming toward the shore. Everyone else had already made it to the other side. As spent as they were, they had no taste for diving back in. Nevitt was on his own. So he took action. He turned around and swam back across the river to East Liverpool and safety. This posed no challenge to him; he had already proven to himself that he could cover that distance. Nevitt ended up swimming over a mile and a half because he didn't believe he could swim a mile. If he had simply trusted his ability, he would have easily made it to the other side.

A Little Horse Sense

There was this guy in Iowa whose car tumbled into a ditch. He called on a farmer for some help, but the farmer said, "You'd need a team of young stallions to pull up that car. I only have one horse, Dusty. He's blind and old. We'll bring him over to the ditch, though, and see what he can do. But don't expect much." The farmer hitched Dusty to the car, snapped a whip in the air, and said, "Pull, Jimmy, pull!" Dusty never moved. The farmer snapped the whip again and said, "Pull, Sammy, pull." Dusty still didn't move. The farmer snapped the whip a third time and said, "Pull, Charley, pull." Dusty remained still. The farmer snapped the whip the fourth time and said, "Pull, Dusty, pull." With one mighty tug, Dusty yanked the car out of the ditch.

The grateful driver shook the farmer's hand and said, "Thanks for freeing my car, but there's something I don't understand. Dusty never moved when you kept calling him by those different names. Why didn't you just call Dusty by his name from the start?" The farmer replied, "I had to call out those three names first. Dusty is blind. If he'd thought he had to do all that work by himself, he never would have even tried." Perception. Don't let yours limit you.

There Are Only Ten Defenders

At the end of the 1960 football season, Jerry Burns replaced Forest Evashevski as head football coach at the University of Iowa. Coach Burns retained me as a graduate assistant. We had a great team. However, our quarterback, Wilburn Hollis, was not the most effective passer I've ever seen. He was a great athlete blessed with a powerful arm. No one could argue that he didn't have a nice touch for the ball. But he lacked confidence in his gifts.

During one pass scrimmage, Coach Burns removed one of the defensive linebackers. Then he called plays that required Wilburn to throw hook passes to the tight end. Naturally, he connected on each one because the linebacker assigned to stop that particular strategy was sitting on the sidelines. Wilburn didn't know that. He never realized there were only ten men on defense for that entire series of plays. The more passes he completed, the more his confidence soared.

As soon as he came off the field, Coach Burns said to him, "See how good you can be when you believe in yourself." It was true. Wilburn Hollis went on to become one of the greatest quarterbacks in Iowa history. I have never forgotten this lesson. Passing a football is like putting in golf. Mechanics are important, but not nearly as important as confidence in yourself and your abilities.

Hot-Dogging Isn't Confidence

Unfortunately, some players confuse hot-dogging with confidence. You'll see players engage in such complex dance steps after scoring a touchdown, you would swear they were part of the halftime show. LaToya Jackson doesn't display some of the moves these guys have. I know many fans find it entertaining, but I think athletes should conduct themselves with decorum.

When our players carried the ball into the end zone, we didn't want them to act as if it was the first time they'd ever been there. Taking a matter-of-fact approach every time you score or make a great play can be more intimidating than any choreographed pyrotechnics. It tells everybody you are accustomed to success. However, I must admit to allowing our players one bit of theatrics. Whenever they lined up for the start of an important game, I wanted them to look into the faces of their opponents and wink. It was our way of letting the other team know we were going to be there all afternoon.

For the most part, though, I have always asked our players to project confidence subtly. If you played for me, you weren't allowed to taunt our opponents. I also didn't want our athletes throwing helmets or displaying exasperation when things went poorly. They have almost always complied with these wishes. And that made us a better team. Never let anyone know you're rattled. They will draw strength from your discomfort.

It was often difficult for me to follow my own principles. I am an emotive person. I had to discipline myself not to get upset when things weren't going our way. I *would* often lose my temper whenever an official made a call I didn't agree with. But, as I explained to my players, that was part of my job. I was doing it for a purpose. Coaches voice their displeasure in the hopes that the call won't occur again. However, I tried to refrain from expressing anger in front of my players during a game. Oh sure, I have yanked a few athletes from the gridiron by their face masks. But that was only if they were fighting or involved in some other unsportsmanlike conduct. Fortunately, those were rare events. If you are a leader and you want your people to remain cool in crisis, you have to set the example.

Next Time Think: Wrestlemania

Of course, I could do my share of dumb things. For instance, Notre Dame was playing Brigham Young University in a hard-fought contest that saw us finally build an insurmountable lead in the game's closing minutes. With time running out, BYU called a pass play. Peter Bercich, our linebacker who currently plays for the Minnesota Vikings, was assigned to execute a delayed blitz on the quarterback. He caught BYU's center off-balance. As Peter exploded past him, the only way the center could stop our man was to grab him in a headlock and wrestle him to the ground. A flagrant holding penalty, I thought. Everyone on the field and in the stands saw it. Everybody except the referee. For reasons known only to him, he refused to throw the flag.

I couldn't believe it! I felt that the fellow who missed the call should only receive half his officiating fee since he was obviously only watching one team. After BYU completed its next pass—more cause for chagrin—I called time out and had the head referee, Tom Thamert, join me on the sidelines. Tom hadn't made the call. However, he was responsible for his crew. I put my arm around his neck in a gentle half-headlock and asked, "Tom, is this a penalty? If it isn't, we need to teach that technique to my players, because it is so much more effective in picking up linebackers than the one we are teaching now."

I had made my point. However, the media treated my demonstration as if I had actually attempted to assault Tom.

You can imagine my dismay that night when I discovered that every national news show was running a film clip of the encounter. I thought the reporters slanted their coverage for the sake of sensationalism. But I could understand their take on the incident. I was at fault because I used poor judgment. My intentions were good; my timing and method were deplorable. You can't beat yourself up when you make a mistake like that. Take the heat, learn from the experience, and move on.

We Are All Part of a Team

Life is a team-oriented experience. Though you rarely think of it, there are thousands of people who work to make your day easier. Where would you be if the farmers didn't produce the milk and vegetables or the postman didn't deliver your mail? You may feel like a lone wolf, but like everyone else, you are dependent on someone. Never lose sight of that.

Handling Pressure

People often ask me how we prepared our players to perform under pressure. I remember when Tony LaRussa, then manager of baseball's Oakland Athletics, requested permission to attend a Notre Dame football practice. Tony's team was in Chicago to play a three-game series with the White Sox; both clubs were involved in a tight pennant race. I told Tony we would love to have him attend our drills provided he observed a rule we had: Any celebrity or former player who watched us practice had to briefly address our team.

Tony not only spoke to our players, he gave one of the best locker room speeches I've ever heard. This is the gist of what he said: Pressure comes when someone calls upon you to do a task for which you are unprepared. If you have to take an important test and haven't studied, you feel the pressure grind as you trudge off to class. However, if you have cracked your books, you are disappointed when you learn the professor has postponed the exam. If I have to make a six-foot putt and I know I haven't spent adequate time perfecting my putting stroke, the pressure as I approach the ball is asphyxiating. But when I know my putting game is sharp, I'm eager to sink that shot. So ultimately, the only pressure we feel is the pressure we place on ourselves.

Preparation dispels pressure because it builds confidence. Salespeople who don't understand how their products work dread inquisitive customers. You can see the fear light up their eyes whenever someone approaches them with even the most mundane question. They feel inadequate. Consequently, when a customer rejects their products, they take the no as a personal affront, a validation of their inadequacy. It's not. The customer is simply telling these salespeople that they haven't sufficiently demonstrated the benefits of their products or services. And they can't do that unless they do their homework. If you are going to sell—and everyone in business sells something—arm yourself with information about your products. Learn as much about them as you can. Then you won't run away from customers; you'll be eager to dazzle them with your expertise.

See the Play Before You Make the Play

On the Friday nights before a game, I would have my players attend a relaxation period. For twenty-five minutes, we would sit in a room and visualize how we were going to win the following afternoon. Everyone left in a positive frame of mind. I never guided a session without asking our players to discard their guilt and anger. I knew how those negative emotions could short-circuit creative energy. I was never quite certain how productive these evenings were; after all, we didn't win every contest. But I do know that whenever we asked our seniors what they most liked about our game-week routine, they invariably placed the relaxation periods high on their lists. If you suffer from chronic negativity, buy some tapes and participate in a guided, positive imagery session. It's like running your brain through a car wash.

Visualizations will also reinforce your motivation. Many times we take up a task with enthusiasm, but then it dissipates. On New Year's Day, we have a laundry list of resolutions and feel certain we can fulfill them. We are even excited by the challenges they pose. By January 15, how many of them have we forgotten? We lose our resolve. I've seen this happen in football and the results are disastrous. Avoid this by recommitting yourself every day. Wake up thinking WIN! What is important, what do you need to accomplish today to come closer to your long-term goals? Then visualize the life you will have once you attain your dreams. Draw as detailed a picture as you can. Let images strengthen your resolve. Remember what the great baseball pitcher Satchel Paige once said: "Don't look back, something may be gaining on you." Always look ahead with wonder, hope, and confidence.

The Power of Faith

Faith is believing in the purest sense. People often say, "Show me proof and I will believe." That's not faith, that's fact. I truly believe that I was placed on this earth for a special reason. I also share this sentiment for every other person in the world.

My faith in God allows me to believe that I am significant. Not any better than anyone else, but just like millions of others I can make a difference if I use my talents and abilities wisely.

And I used my talents and abilities to excel at my God-given purpose—to be a head coach. Of course, the president of the university appointed me. And our players, assistant coaches, secretaries, etc. supported me as their leader if I deserved it. But God gave me the authority to lead. It is because of Him I was able to stay focused on what I needed to accomplish, without distractions from those who praised or criticized me.

I think it is vital that each of us believes that there is a God. I'm not writing this book to convert anyone. When you have a religious faith to call on, you can find solace and guidance during your most troubled moments. You know you're never alone.

While you should never be obsessed with your looks, you should maintain a neat appearance. I've always insisted that our players dress in a suit and tie whenever we traveled. I felt we would only meet so many people a day, but there would be thousands who observed us. They would base their first impressions of us on the way we carried ourselves. This didn't mean our team had to look like a squad of movie stars. I merely wanted each player's appearance to reflect pride.

When you look good, you feel good. When you feel good, you perform better. Keep that in mind when you dress in the morning. Before leaving, check the mirror and ask yourself, "Am I projecting confidence?" Look around your residence. Does this appear to be the home of a person with high self-esteem? Many psychiatrists claim a cluttered, unorganized living space is the product of a cluttered, unorganized mind. Remove the clutter. Take care in how you present yourself to the world.

You must also raise your standards for everything you do. Dr. Martin Luther King once declared, "Your self-image should not come from the job you do but from how well you do your job." He went on to say that if your job is sweeping streets, then you have to sweep them as good as Leonardo Da Vinci painted, Beethoven wrote music, and Longfellow wrote poetry. I think this is advice worth following.

Before choosing an action, ask yourself, "Will this elevate my opinion of myself?" If it doesn't, look for an alternative that will. Explore methods that can improve your confidence. And make sure you carefully read the next three chapters. In them, I will describe how you can enhance your self-confidence, as well as the confidence of others. We will give you a formula for winning every day. You won't have to muddle your way through some complicated theory; the Nobel science committee won't be awarding me any prizes. What you'll find is sound, practical advice that anyone can apply if he or she simply knows how.

It all starts when you ask yourself three questions.

8

CAN I TRUST YOU?

Start building your self-image by viewing it through the eyes of others. Anyone you associate with will want the answers to three key questions regarding your character. They might not openly interrogate you; they will measure your behavior and words. If you can answer yes on all three points, then your self-esteem should climb. You can take pride in being an individual of integrity, loyalty, and compassion. People will gravitate to you, seek your counsel, and cherish your friendship. What could be more fulfilling than that? However, if you answer no to any of these queries, don't panic. No one is going to ostracize you from polite society. You have simply identified a liability. Develop it into an asset.

Looking into the mirror, you must ask the first question, "Can I trust you?" All relationships are based on mutual trust. Without it there is nothing. I've had to place faith in my athletes' skills and dedication; they've had to believe in my expertise. My wife and I have been married for thirty-seven years because we can trust each other. If employees and employers doubt each other's integrity, what do you have? An organization where people spend too much time watching their backs and too little time growing their profits. Consumers must trust that your products and services will deliver as advertised or you are out of business.

People hold those they can trust in high regard. They will lend them money or follow them in a cause on nothing more than a word and a handshake. Choosing to trust someone is easy; you read a person's character and make a decision. Creating trust in others is a more difficult matter. How can you do it?

Do Right

The answer is surprisingly simple: Just do right. Live an honorable life. Do what is right and avoid what is wrong. Early in my coaching career, we established what we called our "Do Right" rules. We based all of them on common sense and civility. Our guidelines required players to, among other things, arrive promptly for practice, obey their coaches, maintain certain academic standards, and comport themselves with dignity. In other words, we asked them to behave like responsible adults.

Everyone should establish his or her own Do Right benchmarks. If you have doubts concerning the difference between right or wrong, consult your Bible or Torah. You will find it is worth the effort. I can't tell you how many talented people I have seen trash their careers because they have neither the discipline nor the courage to behave honorably. They flimflam their way through life. Consequently, they never feel as if they genuinely deserve success. They know they haven't earned it.

Every time a golden opportunity appears, these short-cutters find a way to tarnish it. These are the people who drop passes when they are wide open or "forget" to appear at important meetings. They've never met a deadline they couldn't miss. Afterward, guilt overwhelms them. And that makes them feel better. They think, "I am guilty, therefore I have a conscience, which means I am a good person." Once they comfort themselves, they are free to go out into the world. And screw up again. Which invites another round of mea culpa. These lost puppies just don't get it. They should talk to a fellow I know who, while explaining his belief to some friends, addressed the issue of guilt. "We aren't into it," he declared, "we try to get it right the first time."

That should be your aim. Do Right from the get-go. But when you do blunder, don't dwell on it. You're not alone. We have all done dumb things we later regretted. After you make a mistake, make amends. Do what you can to correct whatever damage you have caused. Then vow to yourself that it won't occur again. Get on with your life. That's why your eyes are in the front of your head instead of in back. So you can see where you are going rather than where you've been.

Trust and Your Bottom Line

I don't care if you sell Coca-Cola, Compaq Computers, or Q-Tips. If you're in business, trust is your best product. Let me give you an example of what I mean by that. Just before embarking on a recruiting trip for the University of Minnesota, I noticed a hole in my shoe. I immediately walked into a Dayton Hudson department store and asked the salesman for a pair of size 9D wing tips. After fetching them from the back, he asked if I wanted to try them on. "No," I said, "I'm running late and I'm sure they'll fit. I always wear a 9D." When I finally laced them up an hour or so later, however, they were surprisingly snug. No problem. I figured walking would break them in. Wrong. By the end of that evening, my foot bore a painful blister the size of a silver dollar. It was only then that I noticed that the shoes were an 8½C.

Normally, I would have returned my wing tips to Dayton Hudson as soon as I got back to Minneapolis. However, I was in a moral dilemma. I had already worn these shoes: The store would not be able to resell them. It would lose money if it agreed to a refund. I wondered if that was fair. Was this the store's error or mine? You could argue that I should have tried on the shoes before walking out with them. And you'd be right. On the other hand, there wouldn't have been a problem if the salesman had given me the proper size.

I didn't know what to do. So I took the shoes to a general manager and explained exactly what had happened. I admitted my role in the mistake. After hearing the story, he accepted full blame for the slip-up. Dayton Hudson replaced my shoes. The store rewarded my honesty; I reciprocated by becoming a loyal customer. I will buy items at Dayton Hudson even when I know I can purchase them for slightly less from a competitor. When you stand behind your products, you establish trust within your customers. You create a bond. That's money in your till.

Every Lie Is the Big Lie

I don't have to tell you right from wrong; most people can instinctively identify proper behavior. I can only tell you what I believe to be right. I believe it is right to be honest. Your parents probably stressed this when you were a child. How many times did they say, "I don't care what you've done wrong, as long as you tell me the truth"? Most parents will tolerate a lot, but they should not tolerate dishonesty. When you lie, you are sending one of four messages:

1.   I don't think you are strong enough to handle the truth.

2.   I am too ashamed of myself to take responsibility for my actions.

3.   I can talk my way out of anything because you are so gullible.

4.   I don't have to be honest with you because I don't respect you.

You are also impoverishing yourself. Geniuses of deception do exist. These men and women prevaricate from cradle to grave without anyone catching on. But few possess their unsavory skills. Most liars eventually pay a price. Get trapped in a single falsehood and you can forsake a lifetime's reserve of credibility. Not even a millionaire can afford to squander that.

Once you've established your good name, maintain it. Never blemish it with a misdeed or false word. If you're tempted to do anything that might sully your reputation, think of this poem that hangs in our family room:

Your Name
You got it from your father,
it was all he had to give,
so it's yours to use and cherish,
for as long as you may live.

If you lose the watch they gave you,
it can always be replaced,
but a black mark on your name, son,
can never be erased.

It was clean the day you took it,
and a worthy name to bear,
when you took it from your father,
there was no dishonor there.

So make sure you guide it wisely,
after all is said and done,
you will be glad the name is spotless,
when you give it to your son.

Penalty Called for Lateness

Every athlete at Notre Dame knew our Do Right rules required them to be prompt. When you're late for an appointment, you are flaunting your disrespect for everyone who arrived on schedule. You are telling them their time has no value. No one has the right to do that. When you agree to arrive anywhere at a specific time, you have given your word. Honor it. It may seem like a small thing, but remember how important it is to concentrate on fundamentals. Think of those people of whom it is said, "He (or she) is always late." Is that someone you would trust or rely on for anything? Is that what you want people to say about you?

True Friends Walk in When Everyone Else Walks Out

Loyalty is another Do Right principle. You owe an allegiance to your family, friends, country, and colleagues. If you don't believe certain people deserve your loyalty, why are you wasting your time with them? Over the past twenty years, a cult of self-interest has developed in this country. Its members pledge fidelity only to themselves. To listen to them, one would think loyalty has become an anachronism. But I believe they are in the minority. Most of us need to know that we can count on others, that our friends and colleagues will rally around when the long knives are drawn.

No allegiance, though, can require you to remain silent in the presence of injustice. We should all speak out against wrongdoing. However, if you are part of an organization, loyalty demands that you first voice your displeasure internally. Give your colleagues and superiors an opportunity to rectify a problem before indulging in public condemnations. Go through the proper channels with your grievances. If that doesn't obtain appropriate redress, then take your case outside. But first establish your credibility. Leave the organization. You can't sit in the same trenches as the people you're attacking.

Disloyalty can shatter or solidify any enterprise. History teaches us that. During World War II, France believed its Maginot Line represented an impregnable defense against the German Reich. Yet the Nazi forces easily breached it to eventually sweep into a Paris enfeebled by Nazi appeasers from within. England, on the other hand, endured the greatest aerial bombardment ever unleashed on a country without surrendering an inch of soil to Hitler. Britain stood fast against the enemy assault because its people put aside their differences to swear undivided fidelity to king, country, and cause. We can survive any travail provided we stick together.

Of course, your definition of loyalty depends on your perspective. For example, an eighty-four-year-old man was lying sick in the hospital. His wife of sixty years sat at his bedside, holding his hand. The gentleman said, "You know, I have been reminiscing about our life. Remember the first year we were married? We had a bad crop on the farm and the bank repossessed half our land. But you encouraged me to keep trying. Next year, we had another bad crop and lost the other half of the farm. But you stuck by me. When I joined the army, you joined the Nurses Corps just to be near me. When I was wounded, you tended me until I got well. After the service, I went into five businesses. They all failed but you hung on. You've always been at my side when things go wrong. Now, I'm here in the hospital, infirm, possibly dying, and you're still here. I can only come to one conclusion. You're bad luck!"

Some Last Thoughts on Trust

There is an ongoing debate over the importance of teaching values in schools. I don't understand it. Over twenty years ago, the Supreme Court ruled that public schools could not post the Ten Commandments on the wall. Teachers can no longer discuss the Golden Rule in their classrooms. Schools are told to lighten their codes of conduct, because it is wrong to make students conform. We have become so nonjudgmental that the lines between right and wrong have become blurred. I'm all for personal freedom, but we must ask how free and at what price? Over the past two decades, teenage pregnancies, abortions, drug use, felonies, homicides, and other acts of violence have risen dramatically. The only thing that has declined in our schools are grades. We have to trust our young people with the future of our country. We give them that responsibility. So don't we have an obligation to provide them with the moral fiber it takes to act decisively and honorably?

I can't blame our young people for being confused. Where are their role models? It sickens me to hear athletes proudly proclaim, "I am not a role model." If children look up to you, you certainly are. In fact, let me pose a question to these players, "Shouldn't we all be role models to each other? Do you no longer have to live honorably simply because you can dribble or throw a ball?" I can remember a time when we trusted our government leaders to set good examples. Today, the general mistrust of politicians is best summed up by the words of the esteemed journalist David Brinkley, who has repeatedly said, "Just the fact that someone wants to run for high public office makes him or her suspect." Isn't that a sad commentary?

I'm not sure how we got in this condition, but that's not surprising. A lot of things baffle me. For instance, in 1930 you could send a letter from New York to California for three cents. A ten-minute phone call between the two states cost twenty-four cents. Sixty-five years later, the price of mailing a letter has risen to thirty-two cents, while that same long-distance call will cost you a buck. So what does our government do? It investigates the phone companies to discover how they determine *their* rates.

Here's another one: We keep hearing that our politicians are eager to reestablish a bond of trust with the American people. Then I read about the government spending over $500,000 to build an outhouse in a national park.

Sort of makes you wonder, doesn't it?

We can only engender trust through our actions. We send many fine people to Washington, D.C.; most of our political leaders are hardworking and decent. But some politicians have to reconsider their values. They could alter the public's often negative perception of our government if they stopped accepting suspect donations, running negative campaigns, and making promises they know they can't keep. In other words, they would rebuild trust if they would just adopt a Do Right policy of their own. We all could. Whenever you are faced with a difficult decision, just ask yourself, "What's the right thing to do?" Use that as your guideline. If every action you take is honorable, everyone will trust you. People of integrity will flock to your cause or organization.

9

ARE YOU COMMITTED TO EXCELLENCE?

The next question you must ask yourself is, "Am I committed to excellence?" You can wallpaper every room in your home with "can-do" slogans such as "First we will be best, then we will be first," but only your actions can lend these words weight. The standards you set for yourself are the real measures of your dedication. You must be willing to give everything you do everything you've got. Don't do this to garner approval. Do it because you respect yourself too much to ever accept anything less than your best efforts.

Self-image can be a powerful motivating tool. Make it work for you. Many times before taking the field for a football game, I've told our players that they can fool the television cameras, officials, fans, media, and their friends, family, and spouses. They can even fool their teammates and coaches.

But they cannot fool themselves.

When they place their heads on their pillows at night, they will know whether they gave it their all or let their teammates—and more importantly themselves—down. Win or lose, if you believe in your heart you did the best you could, you'll be able to live with your results. But if you shortchange yourself with a half-hearted effort and fail, regret will be part of your baggage for the rest of your life.

Here Comes Mr. Jordan

To see how far a commitment to excellence can take you, look no further than Michael Jordan. He is one individual I would want to have on any team I coached, whether basketball, football, golf, or whatever. Game in, game out, Jordan demands optimum effort from himself and his teammates. He can't stomach mediocrity. And while anyone with eyes can recognize Michael Jordan's protean talents, you should know that no one practices harder than this All-Star forward. He's always working to improve his game even though he's already the best player on the planet. I've seen him on-court many times, and he never gives less than his best, regardless of the score or the opponent.

My kind of player.

Woody

Woody Hayes was another sports figure whom I loved and respected. His coaches and players felt the same way. Coach Hayes had an obsession with excellence and couldn't tolerate players who didn't share his commitment. I certainly don't condone everything that Woody did; he and I had different styles. But even his critics never questioned Woody's passion for excellence. However, few people realized how his fervor extended beyond the game he loved. I have seen him upset with athletes who were pulling down B's because he knew they were capable of A's. Woody would tutor these players on his own time until they raised those grades. On the playing field, he wasn't satisfied when a player was named All-Conference if he was convinced this young man had the stuff to be an All-American. In short, Woody never settled; he refused to associate with anyone who did. He never compromised his standards to win friends; didn't care, in fact, if anyone liked him. Woody was completely himself, which is probably why he earned the admiration of nearly everyone he touched.

You Have the Right to Be Obligated

A few years back, the Cleveland *Plain Dealer* was doing a story commemorating the twenty-fifth anniversary of Ohio State's National Championship. Since I had served as an assistant to Coach Hayes on that team, a reporter called me for my remembrances. Toward the end of our interview, he asked, "Coach, what's the difference between the athletes today and the athletes of twenty-five years ago?" I thought for a moment before answering, "The same difference that I see in society today. In the nineties, everybody wants to talk about their rights and privileges. Twenty-five years ago, people talked about their obligations and responsibilities."

Every time you join someone in a marriage, organization, or business, you take on obligations and responsibilities. Every decision you make will affect the others on your team. We have the right to do anything we want to do as individuals (provided its legal), but we do not have the right to jeopardize our teammates' chances for success. Harry Truman said it best, "The freedom to swing your fist ends where the other guy's nose begins." Your freedom to do things haphazardly ends where your obligation to others begins.

You should also remember that when you belong to a team, people no longer see you as an individual. For example, if I work for McDonald's in California and I make a decision to do something that offends a customer, it could have a negative impact on McDonald's franchises throughout the country. How is that possible? Let's imagine that the customer I've angered is a professional speaker. He leaves my restaurant as flame-broiled as one of my burgers. And at every speech he makes around the country, he sautés McDonald's. I'm the one who fouled up, but it's my company that is being cooked. This fellow will create a negative impression of every McDonald's from L.A. to New York. All because of me!

Sounds far-fetched, doesn't it. I mean, what are the odds that you'll step on the toes of a public speaker? Except it happens every day! Studies show that a satisfied customer will tell five other people about your business without prompting. An unsatisfied customer will spread his disenchantment to ten times as many folks. So the next time you are with a client and having a bad day, think about those numbers and the responsibility they imply. That should give you all the motivation you need to provide your customers with optimum service every time out. You should have the same attitude as Joe DiMaggio, the nonpareil centerfielder who led those great New York Yankee teams of the 1930s and 1940s. When asked why he busted his fanny in every game he ever played, Joe replied, "Because you never know. There may be fans out there who are seeing me for the first and only time. I want them to remember me as a player who gave my all."

They Must Become Us

At the University of Notre Dame, we would recruit high school athletes from around the country. They had played in diverse programs under different coaches, each of whom had their own singular approach to the game. When these athletes joined us in South Bend, they thought we would have to adapt to their work habits, standards, and values. I disabused them of that notion immediately. At my very first meeting with our freshmen players, I would say, "Gentlemen, in the comic strip *Pogo*, there was a character who once said, 'The solution is obvious, either we become them, or they become us.' I can assure everyone in this room that we are not going to become you. You must become Notre Dame. I want you to learn everything we do at Notre Dame, how we do it, why we do it. It's important that you learn our methods now so that when you become juniors or seniors you can provide the proper leadership for our younger players. That is essential if we are to enjoy continued success. We did not recruit you to change the University of Notre Dame but to conform to the morals and values of this great institution. You won't change Notre Dame, but Notre Dame is going to change you."

Now some of you may read that speech and accuse me of being a martinet. You may think I was being too rigid. I would disagree with that assessment. I was establishing a standard, setting a tone from day one. We have all seen many great companies and schools fail to pass on their rich traditions to the next generation. They are shortchanging their people. We gave our players something to live up to and few of them ever disappointed us. If your organization or team is performing poorly, perhaps it's because you don't ask enough of your people. Never be afraid to demand excellence. But remember, the standards you establish for others must reflect the standards you set for yourself. No one will follow a hypocrite.

Show the Way: Leadership

Leaders must challenge and inspire. I know that many people today believe that demanding excellence is politically incorrect. We are supposed to accept whatever an individual gives us as the natural expression of his ability and not pressure him or her by asking for anything more. Nonsense.

Leaders are obligated to bring out the best in their people. Most people will not reach their objectives unless you encourage them to take risks. You have to lead them out of their comfort zones. There is nothing more satisfying than knowing you have helped someone do the impossible. If you don't ask much from your team, you'll never scratch their potential. George Patton had the right idea on this. The general once claimed his Third Army could finish one battle, march one hundred miles, and fight another encounter in less than forty-eight hours. When a scoffing British commander said Patton was asking the impossible of his men, the general replied, "That's what we're in business for." Every leader must think the same way.

High Standards Start with You

A few years back, I was lying in bed at the Mayo Clinic awaiting spinal surgery. You better believe I was praying that at least one group was committed to excellence that day: my surgeon Dr. Krause and his medical team. When someone is going to filet your spine with a knife, you hope that person was particularly attentive in class on the day his or her professor covered that region. You want to know that your doctor has thoroughly studied your case and cares about your well-being. And you expect that he or she passed up that cocktail party so as to get a good night's sleep before cutting you open in the morning. In short, you want someone who is committed to excellence. What other criterion is there? You certainly wouldn't hire a surgeon because he submitted the best price for the job. If you were an astronaut, would you want to take flight for the moon in a spaceship built by the lowest bidder? Of course not! You would want everybody connected with the project to be the best in their fields. Demand the same of yourself.

Any time I entered a staff meeting, I always felt I had to be better prepared than anyone else there. I knew my coaches needed to see tangible evidence of my dedication. So I prepared meticulously for each meeting because I knew I would be working a tough audience. My assistants at Notre Dame were, in my view, the best in the entire country. They had to be. We had an obligation to fulfill. I felt any student who came to our university should expect to be taught by a team of elite professors and coaches. If you're in a position to hire, don't be afraid to employ people who are more talented than you. They will inspire you to continually raise your standards.

If you hold a position of authority, you also have an obligation to do all you can to create an environment where others can succeed. Success has always been relative for me. I've seen some athletes for whom miracles were commonplace. Just give them the ball and watch them carry it toward yet another record. Other players had to scratch and fight for every yard they gained. In my eyes, if each played to his maximum potential, one was no more triumphant than the other.

It is particularly important that you never underestimate any individual's capabilities. You won't know if you are extracting their best from them if you do. I've always used a player's accomplishments rather that his failures to weigh his potential. If an athlete was only sporadically brilliant, I did everything I could to make him consistently superior. Those flashes of rarefied skill told me how far we could push him. So, while you should demand more from your ultra talents, you should have the same requirement for each player on your team: Give me everything you have. This means your

third stringers should demonstrate as much dedication as
your starters.

Pretenders Need Not Apply

We can't lower our standards during hard times, we must
raise them. Think of yourself as a company. Production is
high, profits are soaring. Then some mishap occurs. Your
sourcing channels dry up, your distribution network unrav-
els, the judgment in a lawsuit goes against you. Do you stop
demanding the best of your managers and employees? No.
You raise the stakes for everybody. Now is the time you need
peak productivity and creativity, or you'll never get out of this
mess. It's the same in life.

A few years ago, I coached Notre Dame in a climactic
game against Bill Walsh and Stanford University. Coach
Walsh had a high-caliber football team, but so did we. For two
quarters, ours was the team with the gusto. We took the game
to our opponents and led 16–0 just before halftime. Unfortunately, that would be as good as it got. Stanford roared back
to hand us a devastating loss, one that cost us the National
Championship that season. That had been our Holy Grail all
year, our reason for being. Now Stanford had expunged it as a
realistic objective.

Following the loss, I am sure our players expected us to
lower our standards. They thought our practices would
become less grueling. Why exert ourselves when we could no
longer be number one? Even I had entertained that thought.
Wrestled with it throughout a sleepless Saturday night.

The following afternoon, I gathered the team to announce
we would indeed establish new standards for the remainder
of our schedule. Only they would be higher than our previous
benchmarks. "Come Monday's practice," I said, "our coaching

staff will work this team harder than it ever has before." When your organization misses a goal or suffers a loss, you must regroup immediately. Forestall any letdown by reestablishing your purpose.

Our All-American guard, Aaron Taylor, missed those Monday drills with an injury. In his place was a second-string guard who was obviously playing by rote. He had no juice, no fire. I'm not indicting his general character. Perhaps he was experiencing problems at home, in school, or with his girl. Maybe he was just having a bad day. I could understand that. Hey, I'm as compassionate as anyone who's ever appeared on *Oprah*. However, I couldn't afford to condone it. That would be doing a disservice to his teammates.

I halted practice and—in full view of his teammates—said to the left guard, "What gives you the right to jeopardize everybody's chances of success? I don't expect you to be an All-American, but I know that you're capable of playing better than you are. Your failure to do so is hurting your teammates. Forget about me. I think you owe them an explanation as to why you're not giving the best effort possible." Such confrontations are out of character for me. However, I knew I had to get a point across. Not just to him, but to the entire squad.

When this young man was unable to account for his lackadaisical play, I said, "Why don't you just go over to the sidelines and think about it." As he trudged dejectedly off the field, the third-string left guard ran in to replace him, but I said to him, "No, we are going to play without a left guard." My players' jaws dropped. They said, "Coach, how can we play without a left guard?" I answered, "Just pretend he's still there."

They broke from their huddle and set up as they usually did. Our center snapped the ball to the quarterback, who handed it to our tailback. One of our defensive backs came full-bore through the spot left vacant in the left guard's absence. He hit our tailback so hard, he knocked him into the middle of next week. Oh, what a thud! You know that train wreck that opens the movie *The Fugitive*? It didn't have as much crash. I'll tell you, my team had seen many hard hits, but this collision awed them. The entire practice field went silent. Then our tailback started screaming that he couldn't see. That gave me a scare, but he was all right once we turned his helmet around.

Everyone thought this would be the end of my little experiment. But I told them to huddle up, again without a left guard. You should have heard the grumbling then. Various players were muttering how this was foolish, stupid, dangerous, a waste of time? A couple of them questioned my sanity. All music for my deaf ears. We ran another play. Once again a defensive linesman pummeled our tailback. The griping increased in intensity and volume. After the third consecutive play with the exact same result, I was facing an open rebellion. No one wanted to huddle up with just ten men on offense. And our tailback announced that if we were going to call that play one more time, I should be the one who had to carry the ball.

I stopped the practice and asked, "What's wrong with you guys?" They were too upset to respond. Finally, our team captain, their spokesman, said, "What's wrong with us? What's wrong with you, Coach? We don't have a left guard." I looked at them and said, "Well, when did you first notice that?" Now they all looked at me as if I were suffering through the late stages of Alzheimer's disease. The captain said, "How about three plays ago when you removed him to the sidelines." I quickly responded, "Aren't you guys the ones who are hallucinating? You've been playing without a left guard all afternoon. You didn't have a left guard out here. You had a pretender. I'm tired of pretenders. What do you think? That just because someone tapes his ankles, yanks on a pair of shoulder pads, and places a helmet on his head, he's a football player? I want athletes who come to play, who are going to give us a 100 percent effort, 100 percent of the time." Believe me, they got the point.

Woody Allen once said, "Seventy-five percent of life is just showing up." It's a good line, but it's never enough. You must commit to do more than merely occupy a seat. When you join an organization, you assume an obligation to your teammates that you will produce to the height of your capabilities day in, day out. No excuses. If you can't honor that commitment, you're not an employee or a teammate, you're a pretender. We might as well play without you.

That incident involving the left guard inspired our players to rededicate themselves. Notre Dame didn't lose another game for the rest of the year. As a matter of fact, we won seventeen in a row. The last five of these came against nationally ranked teams; our average margin of victory in those contests was 21 points. We played in the Cotton Bowl against an undefeated Texas A&M team and beat them 28–3. And by the way, we played each of those games with eleven men on offense at all times.

There wasn't a pretender in the bunch.

Give Them More Than They Expect

The greater your commitment to excellence, the higher the standards you'll be willing to accept. Conflicts occur when you work with people whose standards differ from yours. For example, imagine you have a history professor who has dedicated her entire life to teaching. She has no hobbies and scant social life. Her shelves are overladen with history books now dog-eared from constant rereadings. If you were to turn on her television, you would find all of the stations have been V-Chipped. All except one—the History Channel.

You attend her class with one goal in mind: to be valedictorian of your graduating class. An A in this class is your goal; anything less will be a crushing disappointment. You invest hours into study and extra-credit assignments. No one in class participates more often than you.

Sitting right next to you in history class is your college football team's quarterback. He also has a driving aspiration: to someday be an NFL superstar. Before he can do that, he has to prove himself to the pro scouts by posting two or three good years worth of college stats. Which means he must stay in school. He does this not because he cherishes academia, but because he needs the showcase for his talents. To remain eligible for his team, our quarterback must pass history with a D. So that's all he aims for—the bare minimum.

Who is the history teacher more likely to get along with and understand? It won't be the quarterback. His standards are so much lower than his teacher's, they might as well be on different planets. That teacher will take only a minimal interest in the quarterback's success. If you want anyone to empathize or ally themselves with you, you must match or surpass their commitment with one of your own.

Another Tip from My Friend Harvey

I've mentioned the sixty-six questions contained in Harvey Mackay's best-selling *Swim with the Sharks Without Being Eaten Alive*. I think his final question addresses any business person's commitment to excellence. It asks, "Do you know as much about your customer as your competitor does?" If you call on accounts without knowing anything about their needs and how you can answer them, you won't sell much of anything. Do your homework! Uncover as much data as you can on your account's business—not merely the side of it that affects you. The advantages of this knowledge are obvious. Suppose a salesperson calls on you and does nothing more than take you through his usual pitch. He knows nothing about the other merchandise your business sells, doesn't even know your customer demographics. How interested will you be in his products or service?

That salesperson leaves without an order. Later that same day, some ball of fire comes into your office. Before she even opens up her sample case, she says, "I know your customers tend to be middle-aged people from a moderate income group. You sell a lot of paperback books here, so they are readers. I have a line of reading glasses that are elegant but inexpensive. Just right for your target customers. Now, I know you've had reading glasses in before and they didn't do well. That was because your display got cluttered and your distributor was inconsistent, so you were often out of the most popular grades. I will service the display personally every week and make sure your orders arrive on time. You have my personal guarantee on that!" Whew! Who are you going to do business with? You are going to sign on with the person who has made a tangible commitment to being the best. All relationships are built on trust; people will believe in you only if you demonstrate that you set high standards for yourself and your products.

Change Your Standards, Change Your Life

As I have said before, you render a disservice to your organization or your people whenever you lower your standards. Notre Dame has always been a special place for a number of reasons. One of them is because the faculty has maintained lofty standards from the moment the university opened its doors. When students come to Notre Dame, they are in the big leagues. That half-hearted effort that may have seen them through high school won't cut it here.

Alton Maiden was one of our players at Notre Dame. Alton was a solid citizen from an upstanding family. However, when he first arrived in South Bend, he was about a dime short in self-dedication. Anyone who talked to him could see he was an intelligent young man, but he was achieving only the bare minimum in the classroom and on the football field. His grade-point average was barely above 2.0.

When he failed to meet the university's academic requirements for two consecutive semesters, he was asked to leave Notre Dame for one year. Many people thought the punishment was too harsh, that the university should be more understanding. But we couldn't coddle Alton or any other student. You see, we loved them too much. When you have someone's best interests at heart, you often have to inflict some short-term pain to lead them to a long-term gain.

Alton understood this. He didn't utter a word against the university's decision. During the twelve months he spent on his personal Elba, he examined his own attitude toward university, football, and life. He returned to us transfigured. Mediocrity was no longer acceptable to this young man. When I welcomed him back, Alton announced that he intended to graduate from Notre Dame and that he would be the best-conditioned player on our team come the fall. He also promised to win the starting middle guard's position.

Talk about raising your standards. Alton had come to us with both guns blazing and he was aiming high. I mean, we believed he could raise his marks. Any intelligent person can do well in school provided he or she commits to the work. Alton certainly had the smarts. But starting middle guard?

Our coaches didn't even think he would be first team; we didn't see him as that kind of player.

Guess who fooled us?

As promised, Alton came to fall practice in better shape than anyone on the team. He won the starting middle guard's position, played every game, provided inspiring leadership, and even scored two touchdowns on defense. And oh yes, Alton maintained a strong B average and graduated Notre Dame. Just like he promised. Upon his graduation, I wrote letters of reference for him to several corporations; I knew he would be an asset to any one of them. Asset? Heck, if Alton told me he was going to work his way up to the presidency of any one of them—I don't care if it was Disney or Microsoft—I'd believe him. He taught me never to bet against anyone who is committed to excellence. It's why when people look at someone who is underachieving and say, "Well, this is who they are; you can't change them," I automatically think, "You're right. But they can change themselves!" Just take a look at Alton.

The Dash

When our Notre Dame team visited Ireland, Alton and the rest of our players visited a twelfth-century cemetery in the rear of a monastery. I don't know if the somber, almost eerie atmosphere inspired Alton Maiden to take up his pen, but shortly after we returned from Dublin, he stood up at our weekly luncheon and read the following poem, which he called "The Dash":

*I have seen death stare at me with my own eyes in a way
   many cannot know.*
I've seen death take others but still leave me here below.

*I've heard many screams of mother cries but death has
refused to hear.*

*In my life I have seen many faces filled with many, many
tears.*

*After death has come and gone, a tombstone sits for many
to see.*

But it serves no more than a symbol of a person's memory.

*Under the person's name it reads the date of birth—and the
date the person passed.*

*But the more I think about the tombstone the only
important thing is the dash.*

Yes, I see the name of the person, but that I might forget.

*I also read the date of birth and death, but even that might
not stick.*

*But thinking about the person, I can't help but to
remember the dash*

*Because it represents a person's life and that will always
last.*

*So when you begin to chart your life, make sure you are on
a positive path*

*Because people may forget your birth and death, but they
will never forget your dash.*

I've never forgotten that piece. It reminds us all that the greatest legacy we can leave behind is a memory of a life lived fully and honorably, a life dedicated to being the best we can.

Sometimes It Takes a Little Incentive

Not everyone will commit to excellence on their own. They need a little persuasion first. For example, there was a rich man in Texas who invited his entire hometown to his mansion for an all-day barbecue. He wanted everyone to see how well he had done for himself. He let them walk the grounds, even browse through all his rooms, but he didn't want them swimming in his built-in pool. So he filled it with alligators—vicious, snapping things that hadn't been fed in over a week.

Well into the evening, the host was a little worse for the wine. He clanged a big dinner bell to get everyone's attention. "I've been looking at my pool of alligators," he slurred, "and thought, since it's hot, some of you might want to swim. So I'm offering to give the deed to my ranch, one million dollars cash, or my beautiful daughter's hand in marriage to whichever one of you hombres can swim the length of that alligator-infested pool." Of course, he didn't think he would lose the bet, because he was certain no one would be brave enough or crazy enough to attempt the swim.

However, as soon as the challenge left his lips, a splash was heard at the other end of the pool. Someone had, indeed, dived into the water. For three minutes, this guy evaded and fought those hungry gators. When he emerged at the other side, bleeding and exhausted, the millionaire grabbed his hand. "I never would have believed anyone could have done it. I'm a man of my word and I want you to pick your reward. What'll it be, son, the mansion, the money, or my daughter's hand."

The guy said, "I don't want any of those things. I want something else." The millionaire was so impressed he said, "Just name it." The guy replied, "I want to know who was the wise guy that pushed me into the pool?"

Who Can You Count On? Discipline

You can't talk about sacrifice without mentioning discipline. Discipline is not what you do *to* yourself; it is what you do *for* yourself. Without self-discipline, we can't make appropriate

choices. Watch the television news. You'll see astronauts floating through space and oceanographers burrowing into the
depths of our seas. Science is teaching us how to master the
land, air, and ocean, yet we seem to have a difficult time learning how to master ourselves. It is the most important victory
we can ever gain! I admire people who have the self-discipline
to do whatever it takes to excel. When opportunity presents
itself, these people act. What happens when opportunity is
not around? They go out and find it. They don't procrastinate.

You can rely on self-disciplined individuals. We've heard
many inspiring slogans over the years, but one of my all-time
favorites is "You can count on me." People must know that
they can rely on you at crunch time. If they can't, what good
are you? However, you cannot help anyone unless you
develop mental toughness. That's where self-discipline comes
in. Unfortunately, too many of us equate discipline with punishment. Just mentioning the word "disciplinarian" can con-
jure a picture of some iron-fisted dictator who metes out retri-
bution to anyone who doesn't follow his or her orders.

I have been referred to as a disciplinarian, but I've never
heard the word as pejorative. For me, a disciplinarian is
someone who requires that people understand the conse-
quences of their decisions. You use discipline to reinforce
choices. Our athletes and my children knew that if they chose
to misbehave, they were also choosing to pay the conse-
quences. For a player, that could mean a benching or even a
suspension. For child, it might mean we would ground them
or deny them certain privileges. In each case, I never pun-
ished anyone; the offenders chose the punishment themselves
by their actions.

Mature people should be able to accept this, provided you
are fair, consistent, and firm. As a leader, you have an obligation to weigh all the facts, to examine any extenuating cir-

cumstances associated with the infraction before coming to a judgment. Consistency requires that you never ignore any individual's violation of your team's rules. Talent is never a mitigating factor. Your All-American running back is just as liable for bad behavior as your third-string kicker. Pick and choose which rules you will enforce with whom and you invite chaos.

For example, in 1988 our nationally top-ranked Notre Dame team was scheduled to meet the second-ranked University of Southern California. Beating USC's Trojans would give us a stranglehold on the number one spot. I was confident going in that we could handle them. However, just before the game, an unfortunate incident nearly disrupted our entire team. Throughout the season, two of our best players had become notorious for their lateness. We did everything to correct their problem. Lectures, counseling, threats, punishment drills—nothing worked. Finally, I told them, "If you are late one more time for any team function, your fault, my fault, your parents' fault, the bus driver's fault . . . it doesn't matter. Should you both suffer heart attacks while trucks run you over, I expect you to limp in here on time. If you don't, you are going to miss the next game. I won't play either of you."

These boys went on their good behavior for about a week. They came to all of our practices punctually. However, the night before we met USC, both players were forty minutes late for the team's pregame meal. That tore it. I didn't want the keys to our offense to miss our biggest game of the year, but when they decided to break our rules, they also decided to miss the game. Now I had to support that choice.

Once it was apparent that the duo wouldn't play, I didn't want them around. We never traveled with tourists, plus there was always the danger that their presence would distract our team from its objective. So the following morning, we put them on the first available flight home. As I watched their plane take off, I experienced my first pang of regret. "Lou," I said to myself, "sticking them on that plane was a big mistake. You should have made them walk back to South Bend."

Would it have been better if I had looked the other way? From the standpoint of winning a single game, undoubtedly. One of those boys was our leading ground gainer, the other our leading pass receiver. You can just imagine how their losses could have deflated our offense. But when you are responsible for an organization you don't make any short-term decisions that can jeopardize your long-term gains. I had no option. They chose not to play in the game when they chose to arrive late. It would have been sinful to show preferential treatment. After issuing the warnings I had, I would have lost the rest of the team if I had handled it any other way. Fortunately, the absence of these two stars didn't hurt us; we won our game. I like to think that the victory was a reward for doing the right thing.

Discipline can improve any organization in so many ways. For example, Notre Dame had a brilliant linebacker named Ned Bolcar. Ned had been one of our top performers and was respected enough to be elected team captain. Unfortunately, an ankle injury sidelined him for an entire spring practice. Our two other linebackers, Wesley Pritchett and Michael Stonebreaker, played well in his absence. When the team reported in the fall, Wes and Michael continued to impress. Ned also played good ball, though he didn't play well enough to take reclaim old position. We had no choice but to begin our regular schedule with Wesley and Michael starting.

It was a trying time for Ned. He played in every game and made valuable contributions, but he didn't start. It's hard for a player who is used to being first team to accept a smaller role. After a great win against Michigan, Ned made a comment during an interview that I considered contrary to our team's best interests. We had a rule on our team. Whenever you were interviewed, you used the opportunity to praise, not criticize. Ned had violated that directive by complaining about his lack of playing time.

I took him aside and explained that I didn't pick the starters; the players did that with their performances. As a team leader, he had to understand the powerful impact his words and actions had on the other players. He got the message; this was a fine young man. After our discussion, Ned demonstrated restraint in all his future dealings with the media. He did everything he could to help our team win. Eventually, he started at linebacker for us and went on to play for several years in the NFL. I am thankful that I have been blessed with players and coaches like Ned who could learn from their mistakes and place the team's welfare before their own. You can't win anything without people like that.

You Can Do It

Underconfidence breeds underachievement. We often fail to fully exploit our gifts because we don't realize we have them. When you doubt your chances for success, it's tempting to quit at the first setback. Your misstep becomes an affirmation of your unworthiness. You don't believe in yourself or your future. I must tell you something. You don't have a future. The future isn't something breathing and alive, just waiting for you to encounter it. You create your future; it doesn't exist until you decide what it should be. Bright or bleak, vibrant or mundane, your life is what you make of it. And the actions you choose now will carry over, because the future is nothing more than an extension of the present moment. Challenge yourself to excel, know that you can, and there isn't anything you can't do. Decide with your whole heart and consciousness that you will make things happen. Once you do, I want to see someone try to stop you. We'll have to reserve a hospital bed for that bonehead in advance, because you will run right through him.

The Proud, the Few

Whenever I watch someone go about their business, I ask myself, "Are they committed to excellence?" When I watch journalists conduct interviews or report a new story on TV, I wonder, "Have they prepared themselves to do their job to the best of their abilities?" I ask the same question when I visit a company or school. You can tell if an establishment is committed to excellence by the way it is maintained. Is the environment clean and orderly? Are the people there delighted to see you when you arrive? Does everyone seem to know what their missions are? Look through an organization and you'll find all the clues you need to measure the height of its standards. Observe, then ask yourself, "Is this an organization with pride?"

Building pride in an organization is integral to its success. It has been my experience that you cannot build pride and esprit de corps if you allow anybody to be a part of your organization without requiring them to make sacrifices. As an army lieutenant, I had numerous opportunities to interact with members of the U.S. Marines. These soldiers took pride in belonging to the Corps; they demonstrated this in their appearance and behavior. They understood that it took superior dedication and discipline to excel in the Corps. Every marine I ever came in contact with conducted himself as if he knew he was a member of the elite.

On the other hand, there are some organizations who only require their members to have pulses. And it you don't have one, they'll grant you a waiver. These institutions remind me of the Groucho Marx line, "I could never join a club that would have me as a member." If you don't demand that your people maintain high performances to remain on your team, why should they be proud of the association? Exacting standards build pride, because the people who survive them know they are among a select few. Don't be afraid to be exclusive.

Drugs: Just Say No

When I was at the University of Arkansas, I had a great football player who had developed several damaging personal habits. His primary problem was substance abuse. He was sabotaging himself. When I saw what they were doing to him, I decided we had to have a drug-testing program in place. When you are on a team, you have to trust that your teammates are capable of playing their best. No one can excel with drugs in their system. Drug testing (and accompanying threat of suspension) provides athletes with an incentive to avoid this dangerous habit.

We started our program at the University of Arkansas in 1982. It wasn't as sophisticated as those that we have today, but it was a start. It enabled us to guarantee to our players' parents that their sons were entering a drug-free environment. Based on my experience, I don't believe anyone can help addicts unless they choose—there's that word again—to help themselves. If they are willing to do that, we must guide them toward professional assistance.

We can ignore the lures of drugs and alcohol if we are committed to excellence. If you are in a place where intoxicants are available, think of your WIN formula. Visualize your goals and ask yourself, "What's Important Now?" As soon as you realize that getting high will hinder rather than help you attain your objectives, you should have no difficulty deciding to leave.

Mr. Knight Makes His Point

In 1970, when I was coaching at William and Mary, our team suffered a rash of quarterback injuries. Despite this, we were still in the hunt for the Southern Conference championship. We were still losing games. However, every week we made a little more progress. You could see these athletes were learning how to win.

During practice, our defensive and offensive teams worked out at opposite ends of the field. I stayed with the defense all morning. After our drills, I walked into our locker room and asked Larry Beightol, our offensive line coach, how his players had performed. He replied, "We had a problem with David Knight." That was a small shock. David, a wide receiver, was a talented young man whom my daughter Luanne absolutely adored. He had never given us any trouble before.

Coach Beightol went on to tell me that David had repeatedly ignored his orders to get into a huddle. I was in no mood to hear that one of our players had deliberately defied a coach. When I sought David out, we had the following exchange:

Me: "What's this I hear that you don't want to get into the huddle?"

David: "No, I don't want to bend over and get in the huddle. Why should I?"

Me: "Why does Boyd Dhaller of the Green Bay Packers get in a huddle? Because Vince Lombardi tells him to do so. You get in that huddle because you are part of the team."

David: "That doesn't help us win!"

Me: "Well, maybe you don't like a lot of other things we do."

David: "As a matter of fact, there are a lot of suggestions I could give you which will improve this program."

That's all I needed to hear. I was boiling now and wasn't about to continue this conversation in front of the whole team. I told David to see me in my office the next day. I knew I would need at least twenty-four hours to calm down. That night David phoned me. I assumed he wanted to apologize. Instead, he announced that he was transferring to another school and wouldn't be making our upcoming weekend trip to play an important conference game.

I asked him why he was behaving in this manner. My question opened the door to a lengthy conversation. As we spoke, I realized David really didn't have a problem with our huddle. His real gripe was that we weren't throwing the ball in his direction often enough. That might sound selfish. It wasn't. David wanted the team to win. He had so much confidence in his prodigious talents that he was certain if we threw more passes his way, we would score more points.

Since David and I shared the same objective—a winning season—I considered his complaint and saw the logic behind it. He *could* help us win and we weren't fully utilizing his talents. Without making any guarantees, I told David we would see what we could do about getting the ball to him more often. For his part, Mr. Knight promised to return to practice and participate in all our huddles. He did play in our game that weekend. Oh, how he played! David caught several key passes, including one for the winning touchdown.

We won the rest of the games on our schedule; David contributed to every victory. And he saved his best for last. During the final game of the season, we were 5 points down with the ball on our own 20 yard line. Only fifty seconds remained on the clock. David caught two passes for 70 yards, then scored the touchdown that clinched our Southern Conference Championship. He would go on to set many of William and Mary's receiving records before starring with the New York Jets in the National Football League.

While David was a free spirit, he was also a highly disciplined athlete. Our confrontation produced a positive result because it uncovered our common aims. Once he knew I was just as committed as he was, David dedicated himself to fitting into the team environment.

It's Bo Calling . . .

In 1989, Notre Dame played its second game of the season against the University of Michigan in Ann Arbor. They were coached by Bo Schembechler, one of the greatest football coaches of all time. I knew it would be a difficult game, but I prepared the team while expecting to win.

Everyone on our team was fired up to play Michigan. We started off the preseason practice with intense focus. By the tenth day, however, our players were exhausted; I could see they were practicing by rote. When you notice your team is phoning its performance in, you must take immediate action or you court sure disaster. Preparation counts for everything! I have always told my players that I can forgive physical mistakes. Missed tackles, missed passes, missed plays . . . they're all part of the game. But poor preparation is intolerable, no matter what profession you are in.

We had to do something to get our practices back on track. So I called the team together before practice and announced, "Men, I called Bo Schembechler today and asked how his Michigan players were faring." Of course, I hadn't really called Bo, but no one on the team knew that. I told them, "Bo said his players were tired. I told him you were tired too, so I offered him a deal. If he would give the Michigan players the day off, I would give our team a day off." The players started cheering and high-fiving each other. I let them celebrate for a bit before signaling for their attention. "Men," I announced, "Bo said no!" The team went silent. "Bo," I continued, "doesn't care how tired you are. They have a tough Big Ten schedule and his players have to be ready for it. He is going to practice two hours today. Now, I don't want to practice you today at all, but if we're going to beat Michigan, we have to start now. They are going to practice for two hours. That means we have to practice for two and a half."

That two-and-a-half-hour practice session ended up taking three hours, but it was a productive afternoon. Our team had reestablished its focus. My talk worked so well, I did a variation on the same theme the next day. Just before we took the practice field, I called everyone together and announced, "Men, I called Bo again today and said, 'I know your players are awfully sore, so let's practice without pads. You put Michigan players in shorts and I'll do the same for Notre Dame.' He turned me down again, boys. Said his players were scrimmaging no matter how sore they were. Men, I don't want to scrimmage you; I do feel your pain. But if we are going to beat Bo we have to scrimmage. Don't get mad at me. Just remember this when you see Bo on September 12."

We had a great scrimmage. So naturally, we received messages from Bo for four consecutive days. On the fifth day, before I could relay the latest missive from Michigan, one of my players shouted out, "Hey, Coach. I called Bo today." I asked, "What did Bo have to say?" He replied, "Bo says his players eat steak and lobster." We all laughed about that and I knew I didn't have to make any more calls to Coach Schembechler. This team was ready. When we played Michigan, Raghib "Rocket" Ismail returned two kickoffs for touchdowns to lead us to a win. At least that's what the following morning's box scores claimed. Actually, we won that game when our players decided they would not allow Michigan's commitment to excellence exceed theirs.

It Wasn't That Hard

I always thought it was crucial to convince our Notre Dame players that they were special and deserved to win. Coaches must coalesce their athletes so they can function as a unit rather than a group of individuals with conflicting agendas. We told our players that we would consistently outwork and out-tough our competition. This meant our practices would be rigorous, so grueling that many of the players would be unable to endure them. This was our challenge to our athletes. They had to prove to us that they could take it, that they deserved to wear the hallowed uniforms of the Fighting Irish.

Our winter conditioning programs started at 6:00 A.M. This immediately got everyone's attention, because January mornings in South Bend aren't warm enough to be called cold. When that alarm clock goes off at 5:30, pulling yourself out from under your toasty comforter to step into the desolate chill takes genuine willpower. Since our boys would be rising much earlier than the average university student, faculty members expressed the concern that they might cut their first classes in favor of returning to bed. So we established harsh penalties for any student who cut class for any reason.

It took a Spartan persistence to get through our workouts.

Today, the players who survived will claim that we had containers on the field so they could throw up their breakfasts without missing any work. That's a small exaggeration. I don't remember anyone regurgitating, but then again I wouldn't have noticed if they had.

Many of our players will tell you Marine boot camps are not as strict as the practice sessions we ran back in 1986. But they paid off. The discipline, the stamina, the mental toughness . . . these are the things you need to out-grind your opponents in the close games. When you play a team of equal physical ability, it comes down to a question of will. Whose is stronger, yours or your opponent's? Let them wilt when you turn up the heat.

Notre Dame's climb back to the top of the college football world started with those winter practices. And you know what? Those were the easiest workouts we held during my Notre Dame tenure. Each year, our drills became progressively harder. But because our players had improved their work habits by raising their standards, they didn't notice any difference.

In fact, even though you still heard the odd complaint, they were proud of what they could endure. They felt ready to confront any task. These men could bare-hand grizzlies by the time we were through with them. And you wouldn't have wanted to wager on the bear in that fight.

They also came away with respect for one another. That is the essence of esprit de corps.

You notice how strangers will rally together in a catastrophe? It's the same principle. Turn your organization into a team by asking them, as well as yourself, to accomplish the impossible. Don't be afraid of coming up short. It is the challenges we overcome that make life rich, that make it memorable. Hey, if David had killed a dwarf instead of Goliath, who would have noticed? Who would have cared?

10

DO YOU CARE ABOUT ME?

O ur final question is, to my mind, the most critical of the three: "Do you care about me?" Everyone you interact with will want to hear a resounding "Yes!" when you answer that question. You should receive the same enthusiastic response from them. Never underestimate the positive effects that love and compassion can have on your family, organization, or team. Creating a caring atmosphere is not a complex task. Simply follow the Golden Rule to treat others as you want to be treated. Or heed those Buddhists who embrace the laws of "cause and effect" and believe that if you want the universe to take care of you, you must take care of it.

When you concern yourself with the welfare of others, you engender loyalty and respect. You create value. And you acquire power. An empathetic voice speaking in a hush can persuade and influence far more effectively than even the loudest invective launched in rage. If your communication powers are lacking, remember the adage, "People don't care how much you know, until they know how much you care."

Love Isn't Lax

Too many people in leadership positions confuse leniency with compassion. They believe it is humane to lower standards and bend rules. They think, "If 70 is passing and Johnny can't score that high on our tests, we'll drop the passing grade to 65. Or 60. Or perhaps we will abolish grades entirely. We don't want Johnny's self-esteem to suffer when he fails a quiz."

Experience has taught me that this attitude is harmful to the person it supposedly benefits and counterproductive for society. It's like giving a shot of whiskey to an alcoholic because you feel bad that he has the shakes. Lower your guard, not your expectations. Open your heart to embrace those whose performances are deficient. Find the time to discover the root cause of their problem. Touch and inspire them to exceed their past results. Whenever leaders lower their standards, they are committing selfish acts. It doesn't cost them anything. They don't have to improve their teaching methods or become better communicators.

But it costs those who are in their charge everything. Taking the time to help someone overcome an obstacle, *that* requires an investment and risk. Should that person fail, you share in his or her loss. And if you're thoroughly engaged, your heart will ache. But how it will soar when you triumph, when you introduce those who have never known a moment of self-love to the best within themselves.

We can never minimize the importance of discipline mixed with love. When you genuinely love someone, discipline is a tool to spur them to greater heights. However, there is a thin line between discipline and harassment. The easiest way to discern the difference between these two is to ask this question: "Will this punishment make this individual a better person, athlete, or student?" If the answer is yes, then you're administering discipline. If the answer is no, then it is harassment. Avoid it at all costs.

If yours is a two-parent home, make sure both of you take responsibility for disciplining your children. Don't make one parent the taskmaster or you risk alienating your children from that person. My father was a bus driver for Blue Ridge Bus Lines. He was often gone from the house on three-day trips. Whenever I would do something wrong or destructive, my mom would holler, "Just wait until your dad gets home and I tell him and he is going to give you the spanking of your life." It reached the point where I never wanted my dad to come home. When he did, after hugging him, I would run and hide. My dad could never understand why I hated to see him return. Don't drive a wedge like that between your spouse and your children.

Words Have Weight

Rhetoric is a weapon. How do you wield it? Do you push a word against a noun to drive a principle or knock over an idea? We often string together phrases to persuade, but persuasion can become coercion. How can you tell the difference between communication and manipulation? Examine your heart. Then examine your interactions with others. The movie star Marlon Brando once said, "An actor is a guy who, if you're not talkin' about him, you ain't talkin'." If you dominate every conversation you have, you're broadcasting that you don't care about anyone but yourself.

Using your rhetoric only for personal gain or self-aggrandizement is the essence of manipulation. It means you don't look at people as individuals; you see them as objects that you obtain or discard depending on your needs of the moment. We all do this to some degree. I know I do it more than I care to admit. We can lose this unattractive habit by engaging in genuine give-and-take whenever we speak with anyone.

If you are one of those who has trouble hearing what people are saying because you're too busy framing a response in your head, clear your brain. Concentrate on the other conversationalists lips. Watch the way they form their words. You will suddenly start hearing them in a new way. Their words, if they are at all interesting, will touch deeply and evoke responses you never imagined. Every conversation will become an adventure. Hey, isn't that a good enough reason for you to flap your gums a little bit less?

You can teach your younger children good communication skills by asking them questions and listening to what they have to say. This may require some patience on your part. Whenever we sat down for dinner, I would ask my kids, "What happened today?" My question was usually greeted with silence. So I would say, "Oh, surely something exciting happened to you today." Then one of them would respond, "Nothing." So I'd let it drop until our next dinner, when I would ask the question again—and get the same nonresponse.

This didn't deter me. I knew these young people would open up as soon as they trusted that I legitimately cared about their answers. Sure enough, one day I asked the question and each one of them told me at least one thing that had happened during the day. As the weeks went on, they couldn't wait for our nightly discussions. I didn't even have to ask the question to get them started. Then, the most amazing thing happened. I sat down at the table and before I could say a word, one of my children looked at me and said, "Tell us about the exciting things that happened to you today." Communicating with your children is easy if you genuinely care enough to work at it.

The Kindness of Strangers

I guess I'm still enjoying my fifteen minutes of fame, because people still ask me for my autograph. Sometimes they also want to have a photo taken with me—which I find even more baffling—or to engage in a little chit-chat. I never refuse a request if I'm seated. However, when I'm on the run or my hands are full, I don't always comply, unless the request comes from a child. Personally, I have no idea why any grown-up would want my name on a scrap of paper. I tell them my signature is worth nothing today, but if they hold on to it for five years, it will be worth twice as much. You think I'm kidding? I once looked up the price of my autograph in a collector's guide. It was the only autograph listed that had a negative value. If you owned it, you owed someone money.

I always try to be cordial when I'm approached. I give autograph seekers my respect and attention. Then one day, I realized I treated these strangers—for that's what most of them are—with more patience and understanding than I did my own family and friends. Did that twist my head around! I made a vow that from that point on, if I was going to be so concerned with making a good impression on people, I would start with those I loved the most. It's something we should all consider. We should treat everyone in our lives as if they are our most important customer. Just think what a better world this could be.

Make Yourself Incomparable

Never compare yourself with anyone. What's the point? If a person is doing better than you, it doesn't take money from your pocket. Whatever portion of success they own wasn't stolen from you. On the other hand, if seeing someone in diminished circumstances makes you feel better about yourself . . . gee, do you need a priority check.

I'm always amused and saddened to see the turmoil people put themselves through by comparing themselves to others. They are playing mind games. Just think about it. Say you're job-hunting with the hope that you can find a position that pays $40,000 a year. At that moment, this represents so much money to you, you wouldn't know what to do with it. After numerous interviews, a top firm hires you. For $65,000 a year. Wow! You're in heaven. You got all that you wanted and more. Then, the following week, the firm hires someone with the same background as you for the same position. Only they agree to pay her $75,000 annually. What are you going to do, slide into doldrums? You were ecstatic a week ago and nothing in your life has changed. Her salary doesn't come out of your pocket. Find your happiness within.

Comparing myself to others has never worked for me. I often tell this joke to illustrate my feelings toward comparisions: "When I left Notre Dame, the administration asked, 'What can we give you?' Instead of consulting my own desires, I asked, 'What did you give Ara Parseghian when he left?' They replied, 'A golf club.' I thought, 'Ara was on the cover of *Time* magazine, and all they gave him was a measly golf club?' So I said, 'Just a handshake and your thanks will be fine.'" I wasn't being magnanimous; I just didn't need another golf club. Of course, later on I discovered the golf club they gave Ara had thirty-six holes on it. See what I mean about comparisons! They'll mess you up all the time.

The Woody You Didn't Know

Let me share a secret with you: Woody Hayes loved people. Yes, he could be cantankerous and short-tempered, but that was because he was a perfectionist. He demanded the best from himself and everyone around him. If you gave him less than that he could be, well, testy. But he was also capable of incredible acts of warmth and kindness. You never heard much about them, because Woody never performed his good deeds under a spotlight.

For example, did you know that Coach Hayes visited our armed services several times in Vietnam? Whenever he went over there, he usually returned with messages from over 2,000 servicemen. He would personally call each of their families to pass on their tidings. Coach Hayes paid for those calls out of his own pocket at a time when he was only making $25,000 a year as head coach of Ohio State. The expense never mattered. Woody didn't care about money; he cared about people. He continually turned down pay hikes so that the raises could instead be passed on to his assistants. Coach Hayes's family was full-grown. Most of his assistants—including yours truly—were still raising theirs. He reasoned they needed the extra capital more than he did.

When I left Ohio State, Coach Hayes told me if I ever needed anything, just call. He was often the first person I phoned when I had a problem, though I most often called him just to shoot the breeze. However, he eventually stopped returning my calls. So I phoned him and told his secretary, "Would you please tell Coach Hayes that I have a problem and that I need to talk to him." Almost immediately after I hung up, my phone rang. Coach Hayes. He asked me what my problem was. Before I would tell him, I asked *him* why he had stopped returning my calls. He answered, "You don't need to tell me what a good job you are doing or how much the alums love you. You have enough people doing that. I'm returning *this* phone call because you have a problem and I'm here to help." This was typical of Coach Hayes. He disliked small talk.

Woody had no patience for socializing either over the phone or in person. But if you were a friend in trouble, the Marines couldn't get to your side any faster.

Some more examples of the type of individual he was: After he hired me as an assistant, Coach Hayes never again passed through my hometown without calling or visiting my mother to find out how she was doing. It's called thoughtfulness, and we need more of it. Whenever I needed a presenter at a banquet, Coach Hayes would do the honors. Never turned me down.

When I left Ohio State to become head football coach at William and Mary, he was not particularly pleased. In retrospect, I can understand why. It was July, not an appropriate time for a coach to leave a university whose football program was about to go into full swing. Several people tried to talk me out of leaving. We had never lost a game while I was an assistant at Ohio State; they said I should experience at least one loss under Coach Hayes. They talked as if it would be one of the most memorable moments of my life. Apparently, the eruption of Vesuvius was just so much white noise compared to one of Coach Hayes's post-loss outbursts. Somehow, I'm not sorry I missed that.

I took the job at William and Mary because I didn't know if I would ever get another chance to be a head coach. Once Coach Hayes accepted that, he asked me to do one favor for him before I left. He was in the process of writing his book, *Hot Line to Victory*. Coach wanted me to pen the chapter on defensive backfield play. Because of his publisher's deadline, this section had to be completed before I left town.

I wrote the chapter as quickly as I could. This was to be a tribute to Coach Hayes, a thank-you note for everything he had done for me. I finished it well in advance of the deadline and eagerly raced to his office to drop off the material. I will never forget what happened next. He took the manuscript and read it immediately. Coach Hayes never asked me to sit down, so I just stood for what seemed like the longest twenty minutes of my life. I so much wanted to please this man. As soon as he finished reading, he nodded affirmatively—high praise indeed from the Coach—and pulled out his checkbook. He said, "This is fine. I want to reward you for your efforts." He then made out a check and shoved it into my hand.

Well, this would have ruined everything. I didn't want to be compensated and I hadn't done this as a favor. This was a debt of honor for me. I tried returning the check to him, but he refused to accept it. I threw it on his desk and walked toward the door. Before I could get there, Coach Hayes whirled me around from behind and shoved the check into my shirt pocket. When I tried to pull away, he inadvertently ripped the pocket from my shirtfront. The check drifted to the floor and landed between us. I ended this burlesque by picking up the check and tearing it into small pieces. "Coach," I said, "I appreciate everything you have done for me. There is no way I could ever repay you. You can write a hundred checks, but I guarantee I can tear them up a lot quicker than you can sign them." He said, "Okay. You leave me no other option." We shook hands and I walked out of his office. It was my last official act as an assistant coach under Woody Hayes.

On the way home I did have one regret. I was going to William and Mary with our fourth child due at any time. I didn't have an awful lot of money and Coach Hayes had just ripped my best shirt. So I thought, "I wished I had at least looked at the check." Then I put it out of my mind. Coach Hayes could have written it out for $1 million; I still would have torn it up. You can never put a price on friendship; you can never ignore the debts you owe to others.

Keep Your Matches Handy

When I was working under Coach Forest Evashevski on a graduate assistantship from the University of Iowa, he said something to me I've never forgotten. I was in Iowa City just before the start of our Easter vacation. The assistant coaches and I were evaluating game footage when Coach Evashevski joined us. In fact, he sat right next to me, which he didn't often do.

As we sat there watching the film, Coach leaned over and asked, "Lou, are you going to go home to see your girlfriend for the holidays?" I have no idea what prompted that question. As you may remember from a previous chapter, Beth had broken our engagement just before I took my position with Iowa. We had since reconciled, but hadn't set a definite date for our wedding. This bothered me, but I hadn't let on to anyone. Somehow, I believe, Coach knew. He never said much; he took in everything.

I flippantly replied, "No, Coach, I'm going to stay here and let her eat her heart out." Coach gave me a stern look, then thought for a moment before replying. You could see he was measuring his words. Finally, he said, "Lou, absence to love is like air to fire. A little bit stimulates it; too much puts it out. Don't put out that fire."

Well, when Coach Evashevski spoke, it was Smith-Barney time. I took every one of his words to heart and headed home that very night. Good thing I did, too. Beth and I were so happy to see each other, we scheduled our wedding for the following July 22. From the day we were married, I've always made it a practice never to stay away long enough to extinguish my wife's flame. Show people you care by keeping their fires lit.

Wedding-Bell Blues

There will be times when you must say no even though it injures someone's feelings. Such a moment occurred to me just before my wife and I were married. As we were going over our wedding plans, I asked her who would be taking our pictures. Beth said, "Your father has volunteered."

Dad!

I swallowed hard. My father had an intense interest in photography. He had a room filled with camera equipment, all professional-quality stuff. Any time some new lens or other gizmo came out, Dad would buy it. He loved taking photos and brought great enthusiasm to his hobby. Dad knew how to pose people, could tell you what type film worked best under which conditions. There was only one problem: *He took lousy pictures!* No matter how he angled his camera, his photographs never seemed to be quite in focus. When I told Beth how bad he was, she thought I was exaggerating. So I said, "If you don't believe me, look around my parents' home. You'll see pictures we bought from the church or Woolworth's. But you won't see any examples of Dad's work displayed. His pictures are not fit for public consumption."

Beth still wasn't convinced. She said, "It will really hurt his feelings if we say no. He wants to do it and I'm not going to be the one to turn him down." So who did that leave to do the dirty work? The soon-to-be prodigal son, that's who.

To be honest, Beth was right to pass on this responsibility to me. After all, it was my father we were talking about. I was the one who had raised the objections to his photographic skills. I was the one who thought we shouldn't let our wedding pictures—mementos of a glorious day that we would want to cherish with our children and grandchildren—into the hands of an amateur. Our parents would want to look at the pictures over the coming years. They wouldn't want an album filled with fuzzy shots that no one could identify. I was making decent money and could afford to hire Olan Mills, the best photographer in East Liverpool. Wasn't it in everyone's interests that I hire a pro? Of course. There was, however, one other problem. I couldn't tell Dad, either.

So Father did indeed take our wedding pictures. They were a disaster. Only one photo survives from that afternoon: a hazy Polaroid snapped by some guest. This occurred thirty-seven years ago, and I still regret that I didn't have the moxie to say no. If something is important to you, don't make the same mistake.

In 1982, my oldest daughter, Luanne, was preparing to marry Terry Altenbaumer, a University of Arkansas graduate with a chemical engineering degree. I had never married off a daughter before, so I wanted this to be special day for them. I sat down with Luanne and said, "Honey, I love you. I want you to have a great wedding. Whatever you want, we are going to do, because I only plan on marrying you off once. I don't expect this to happen a second time."

I set aside what I thought was a substantial budget for a large wedding. I had to. Since I was head football coach for Arkansas, everyone in the state seemed to believe that they should be invited. Six months before the marriage, my wife came to me and said, "I think it's going to cost twice as much as we had anticipated." "No problem," I said, "I promised Luanne the best." We doubled the budget.

Three months later, Beth came back to say, "I'm afraid our budget isn't nearly enough. The guest list keeps growing and when you add flowers, photographer, bands—" I interrupted her. "Bands?" I asked. "Such as in plural?" She said, "Oh yes. We have to have two bands for dancing so there won't be a lull in the wedding when one of them takes their break."

I thought about all the added expense for another week before approaching Luanne and Terry to say, "Honey, I want you to have anything you ever wanted for this wedding. I don't want you to have any regrets after it's over and I want it to be one that you can really remember with pleasant thoughts. No matter what this wedding costs, I am going to pay the bills and I will do it happily. However, I have been calculating and I believe the two of you can have a beautiful wedding for this amount." I named a figure, then continued. "If you exceed that figure, even by several thousand, don't worry. I will cover it. However, if the wedding comes in under budget, I will write you a check for the difference between what you spend and that figure. You can do anything you want with the money."

I never saw such a complete reversal in plans in my entire life. I mean, they started talking about playing records at this function instead of hiring a band. They became so cost-conscious, I thought they would ask their friends to bring their own meals to the reception. Luckily, they didn't go quite that far. Luanne and Terry had a beautiful wedding with most of the trimmings, but nothing excessive. During the reception, I handed them a check that they eventually used to make a down payment on their home. I didn't make this offer to save money. I did it because I loved these two fine young people. I was going to spend the money one way or the other. I wanted them to choose which would make them happier. When you love people, you don't just blindly do whatever they ask. You identify all their options for them so they can make informed decisions.

Don't Hide Your Love

After my wife finished her first round of cancer therapy—three radiation treatments daily, five days a week over seven weeks—my family was delighted to have her back with us. She had been quite ill and we wanted to show her how much we cared. On the day she came home, we had signs up every-where including a huge billboard that read, "Welcome Home, Beth Holtz. We Love You and Missed You. Your Family and Friends." The numerous yellow ribbons we put around the trees in our yard served as exclamation points for our feel-ings. Looking back on that joyous event, I wonder why more of us don't celebrate those we love every day.

Don't wait for a crisis to show someone you care; demon-strate your feelings at every opportunity. We can so enhance our lives if we understand that everyone we meet is asking, "Do you care about me?" Answer them with some tangible demonstration of your affection. You don't have to erect a bill-board to proclaim how much you care. Just be thoughtful. Always consider the sensitivities and needs of others. Your life has an impact. Be aware of how your actions hinder or help. And, oh yes, don't forget to say "I love you" to someone at least once every twenty-four hours. Its a hyacinth for the soul, yours and theirs.

Everyone Needs a Hugger

One of my fondest Notre Dame memories occurred when we held the 1987 International Special Olympics in our football stadium. Six thousand Special Olympians traveled from all over the world to participate in these games. Each one of them was physically challenged, yet I didn't see a single bitter or negative individual among them. I participated in the event as the official hugger for Lane Three. No matter who ran in that lane or where they finished—first, last, or anywhere in between—my job was to wrap him or her in a big hug and say, "I'm proud of you and I love you." Wouldn't it be nice if we all had a hugger? If we came home every night to loved ones who would wrap us in their arms and say "I love and appreciate you," wouldn't this world be a better place? There is one way to establish this ritual in your home.

You hug first.

We All Have Problems

Diogenes could find an honest man before you could uncover an individual that doesn't have at least one problem. When we think of those in need, our minds automatically turn to the homeless or impoverished. But I have met many wealthy individuals who woke up every morning famished for love, understanding, and encouragement. Never take for granted that success guarantees happiness. Demonstrate compassion for everyone. Especially those who seem callous or spiteful. They probably ache more than you can imagine. Their caustic behavior is a shield for their emotions. Give them a kind word and see if it doesn't improve their demeanor. I guarantee it will do wonders for yours.

As I write these words, I feel some guilt because I haven't practiced this philosophy as often as I should. I don't regret any effort I've ever made on behalf of others, but I do regret those times when I missed the chance to make a positive difference in someone's life.

Get Off Yourself

Nothing upsets me more than seeing people with talent, health, intelligence, and other advantages complain about some petty annoyance. Before you gripe about anything, weigh your blessings. Most of us are more fortunate than we realize; we should express our thanks for that by helping others who are less gifted. Volunteer your time at your local community center, record books on tape for the blind, work at a hospital once a week . . . do something. Extending your hand to others is a wonderful antidote for self-centeredness.

Pass the Kindness Along

One evening during my junior year at Kent State, I received a phone call from my parents asking me to come home the following weekend. There was a personal matter that needed my immediate attention. Neither of them would reveal what the problem was, but I was fairly certain it was of a financial nature.

Since I didn't have the price of a bus or train ticket, I traveled by thumb—or hitchhiked, for those of you who have never rode the Vagabond Express—all the way back home. The trip took several hours. When I walked through the door late Friday night, my parents informed me of their intention to divorce. I felt as if someone had smacked me in the middle of my forehead with a poleax. Since I was living on campus, I had no idea that the differences between my mom and dad had become so wide that they could not reconcile them. All marriages go through difficult times, but I thought my parents' union was secure.

But turmoil there was and it was right there in the living room with us. I spent the weekend as a spectator to the dissolution of my parents' marriage. Had I been prepared for this before I came home, I might have handled it better. But the announcement was such a complete shock, I wasn't sure what to do. I wanted to comfort both of them, but Lord, I didn't want to be in the middle of this. The last thing I needed was for either Mom or Dad to accuse me of taking sides.

By the time I left their home on Sunday evening, I was distraught. You can genuinely care about people without condoning their actions. I couldn't understand why anyone would get a divorce after twenty-three years of marriage. I had to hitchhike back to Kent, and it was the bleakest trip I've ever taken. I also had an important exam scheduled for Monday, and I hadn't devoted a single minute to study. It was an hour before I caught my first ride, a businessman going to Warren, Ohio. He let me off at the intersection of Route 5 and Exit 14, near the turnpike. This was not a route I normally traveled; it left me some thirty-five miles from Kent State. So I walked over to a straightaway and waited for another ride. For two hours. Not a car stopped. Then it started to snow.

I was freezing, but had noticed a restaurant about fifty yards to my left and behind me. Unfortunately, when I patted my pockets, I discovered I didn't have a dime. I just stood there shivering, feeling as if no one in the world cared whether I lived or died. Two more hours passed. Night was falling, the snow was accumulating. Four inches must have fallen by then, and I wondered if I wasn't in for one of our famous Ohio blizzards. I started thinking of that line from the song "Born Under a Bad Sign," the one that goes, "And if it wasn't for bad luck, I wouldn't have no luck at all." Tell me about it.

Finally, a car slowed down as it approached me. I thought, "Thank goodness, a ride at last." Keep singing, folks, my luck was nothing but consistent. After passing me, the car pulled into the restaurant parking lot. Two passengers got out and went inside. They didn't seem to even notice me. Now I was completely depressed.

It would be two hours before I saw them again. They were leaving the restaurant and about to pull onto the throughway when the driver rolled down his window. "Where are you headed, Son?" I told him. He said, "Not too many people are going to be driving in this weather. Snow's not supposed to let up till morning. You'll never get a ride. Hop in. We better take you the whole distance." They went out of their way to help a stranger. It was two and a half hours before we arrived at Kent. After dropping me off, they had to turn around and drive back to where we had started. I had been too shy and cold to get their names. Still don't know who they were. But before they rode off, I shook their hands and said, "I wish I could do something to repay you." The driver smiled and said, "There is. Someday do a favor for someone else and think about us." I have tried to do exactly that as often as possible. Whenever anyone performs a kindness toward us, we have a debt, an obligation to pass that generosity on to others. When it's time for you to leave this life, make sure your account is marked "Paid In Full."

I want to end this chapter with a gift for you, a poem that hangs in the Holtz's home. It beautifully sums up everything I've discussed in this section. It's called "Anyway."

Anyway
People are unreasonable, illogical, and self-centered.
Love them anyway!
If you do good, people will accuse you of selfish ulterior
   motives.
Do good anyway!
If you are successful, you will win false friends and true
   enemies.
Succeed anyway!
The good you do today, will be forgotten tomorrow.
Do good anyway!
Honesty and frankness make you vulnerable.
Be honest and frank anyway!
The biggest person with the biggest ideas can be shot down
   by the smallest people with the smallest minds;

Think big anyway!

People favor underdogs but follow only top dogs.

Fight for underdogs anyway!

What you spend years building up may be destroyed overnight.

Build anyway!

People really need help, but will attack you if you help them.

Help them anyway!

Give the world the best you have and it may kick you in the teeth.

Give the world the best you've got anyway!

—AUTHOR UNKNOWN

11

INTO THE END ZONE: TURN YOUR QUESTIONS INTO VICTORIES

Whenever someone accuses me of being "too country"—which is something I often hear—I usually respond, "That's just fine with me." When I think of the term "country," I think of people who use common sense and keep things basic. I wrote this book, and particularly this final chapter, with that approach in mind.

I am convinced that you will succeed in life if you can answer yes to the three questions we posed in the preceding chapters. Whether we are talking about managing people, raising a family, or improving ourselves, we must establish our integrity, love, and commitment before we can accomplish anything. If you are still not persuaded, think about the individuals you most respect. I'm willing to bet you consider each of them credible, dedicated, and compassionate.

Now think of someone you don't admire and ask yourself the three questions. Does this individual demonstrate genuine concern for your welfare? Is he or she committed to excellence? Would you take his or her word as gospel? You are more than likely to discover that this person comes up short in one or more of these areas.

Sounds too simple, doesn't it? I'm sure it's difficult to believe that three questions can reveal so much about some- one's character. You don't need to have someone lie on a couch for $150 an hour while some therapist digs through the layers of his or her psyche to find out who they are. The answers to those three queries tell you everything you need to know. You can use them to pinpoint any problems you have in your relationships with your family, friends, or associates.

For example, if you had a spiky association with some fel- low in your office, you would first apply the three questions to him to discover if he is the source of this friction. Ask yourself:

1. **Do I trust him?**

If not, why not. Has he ever lied to you? Will he take ethi- cal short cuts? Does he speak in "lawyer-ese," using deliber- ately vague, misleading, or ambiguous language.

Specify the reasons for your mistrust.

2. **Is he committed to excellence?**

You can tell if someone places their maximum effort behind every task. Is this fellow a workhorse or a shirker? Is he the last to arrive at the office and the first to leave? Does he immediately blame others when anything goes awry or does he assume responsibility for his mistakes? Compare his work habits with those of his colleagues and see how he stacks up.

3. **Does he care about you?**

Each person will have his own criteria for this one, but generally, you can tell if a person cares about you if they demonstrate respect for your opinions and feelings.

Once you've put him under the microscope, it's your turn.

Put aside any agendas you have and examine yourself through his eyes. Reverse the three questions:

Have you given that person a reason to trust you?

Have you demonstrated your commitment to excellence for him?

Have you shown how much you care about him?

Every no you receive to any of these queries is a beacon that sheds light on the problem and its solution. For example, if you discovered you doubted this gentleman's dedication, you would list examples of his slipshod approach to his job. Then ask him to meet with you for a one-on-one session to clear the air.

(Of course, if you came up with a trio of yes's when you asked your questions about him, but elicited one or more no's after turning them on yourself, you don't need to have this conversation. You're the one with the problem, not him. Prepare to do some work on yourself.)

Begin that discussion by acknowledging that the two of you do not interact well. State the reasons behind your displeasure, but don't frame them as accusations. Instead, cite the specific examples of his behavior without attaching any judgments to them. Make him see himself though your eyes. One way to encourage this is to admit any failings your questions revealed about your own conduct.

If I were in your place in this instance, I would sit down with my colleague over a cup of coffee and say, "You and I don't get along. I know I haven't given you enough feedback in support of your work. [In other words, I haven't adequately demonstrated how much I care about his needs.] You probably have other complaints about me and I want to hear them. For my part, I've been put off by your recent behavior. You

have finished each of your last three reports past deadline,
which meant I could not start my work on time. You've shown
up late and unprepared for every meeting we've had this
month. And you are way behind this quarter's new client
quota. It doesn't look to me as if you're giving this job your
best effort. What do you think?"

What have you done with this opening? You have put
everything, including your own behavior, on the table without
being overtly confrontational. Instead of presenting random
complaints colored by emotion—always a sure way to ignite a
brouhaha—you have presented a dispassionate litany of specific facts to which this gentleman must respond in some
manner. And you've invited him to present his version of
events.

If he is willing to discuss the situation, give him center
stage. Hear everything he says with an open mind. You may
discover things aren't quite as they seem. There could be
extenuating circumstances behind his behavior. Show a willingness to help him work through any issues. Listen objec-
tively to his complaints against you. Direct the three questions at yourself again to test the validity of these criticisms.
Remember, you're not looking to score points against this
man. Use this dialogue to resolve your differences.

Despite your good efforts, it is entirely possible that the
gentleman in our example may be unreceptive to your over-
tures. Many of us abhor hearing a litany of our shortcomings,
no matter how diplomatically someone presents them. He
may very well tell you where to go before storming off. If he
does that, you must gently point out how unproductive his
behavior is and again give him the opportunity to tell his side
of things.

If your attempts at resolution fail, you have two choices.
You must either decide to accept his behavior (in the event

that his performance is so outstanding in other areas, you can ignore his foibles) or, if the situation is intolerable, arrange a divorce. One of you will leave the department or organization. However, I recommend much soul-searching before you even mention the separation option. Make sure it is what you desire. Once you threaten to go that route, it is usually impossible to reverse field.

I've used a colleague for this example, but you can apply the three questions to any group or individual you're in conflict with. You can also use them as self-examination tools to ferret out the weaknesses in your own character. Once you've identified your liabilities, you can work toward eliminating them. Three questions. They aren't magic. But if you answer them with courage and honesty, they can make most of your troubles vanish into thin air.

A Last Word from the Locker Room

Throughout my career, I have tried to teach life rather than football. I believe everyone has the potential to be a champion. As you enter a new phase of your existence, treat it as if it were a game. It should be enjoyed not feared, fun not work, played not endured, a reward rather than a punishment. There will be times when everything goes smoothly. There will be other moments when you feel as if you are climbing straight up Mount Everest while wearing combat boots. Whatever happens, don't deviate from your game plan:

1.   Maintain a positive attitude.

2.   Welcome adversity as a learning experience.

3.   Act boldly; go for the big play when you're behind.

4.   Review your fundamentals; eliminate any shortcuts.

5.   Think WIN!

6.   Adapt to change.

7.   Give your best effort at all times.

8.   Willingly make the sacrifices that winning demands.

9.   Consider both sides of your three questions.

10.   Remind yourself that the difference between champ and chump is U.

And remember the words of Oliver Wendell Holmes: "What lies behind you, and what lies ahead of you is of very little importance when it is compared to what lies within you." If love, trust, and commitment lie within you, yours will be a happier, more productive life. No matter what obstacles confront you, you will find a way to win. Every day.

AFTERWORD

When I consented to write this book, I knew it was normal procedure to have the author write an auxiliary chapter for the paperback edition. However, little did I realize I would be the head football coach at the University of South Carolina when this happened. Our lives may take strange turns, but I am convinced we can cope with these challenges if we follow the "Game Plan for Success." I can assure you that our program at the University of South Carolina will follow the principles outlined in this book.

My Return to Coaching

When I left the University of Notre Dame, I never felt I would coach again, because where do you go from Notre Dame except, according to my mother, directly to heaven to sit next to the Pope? I enjoyed working for CBS. It is a great organization with very talented people, and I am better prepared to cope with the problems that life presents on a daily basis because of my association with them. Among many things I learned was to appreciate the role of the media. Previously, I labored under the misconception that the media showed up for press conferences and relied on the coach to supply them with information for their newspaper articles. I now know that nothing could be further from the truth. Just as in coaching, business, or any other occupation, you must do your homework if you want to be great. I now realize that greatness requires a commitment, and there are no exemptions.

When you awaken tomorrow and don't want to get out of bed because there are so many problems facing you, get down on your knees and thank God for these opportunities. It is wonderful that you have to get out of bed and accomplish things because people are counting on you to contribute to their success. I have now found out that this is a basic requirement for life and happiness. If you have no reason to get up in the morning, your self-image deteriorates. You tell yourself you aren't important and that no one needs you. This feeling can only be erased if you have dreams and goals that are important to you.

This was an important reason why I chose to return to coaching. Perhaps the most important reason was the encouragement I received from my wife to do so. I had turned the job down three different times and had gone to Nashville to prepare to be the analyst for the NFL game, Tennessee vs. Baltimore. As far as I was concerned, the South Carolina situation was a dead issue. My wife called me in Nashville and said that Dr. McGee had called once again and that she felt I should reconsider my decision. Beth informed me that she had talked to Skip, and he hinted that he would join me because he wanted his children to get to know their grandmother on a daily basis. This was an important factor in my decision. I knew he would be making a sacrifice financially and professionally, but I was also very proud of him. It is important to note that we are proud of our other children as well. We have always believed our priorities as a family should be our faith, our family, our profession, and then our social obligations. Skip had done a great job at the University of Connecticut and had just concluded his fifth season being ranked #4 in the country while winning ten games. This was impressive when you consider Connecticut had never won more than eight games in a season (Skip had tied this record before breaking it). They had never made the playoffs and had never finished in the top ten. I know Skip had a lot of reservations about leaving the University of Connecticut because of his love for his players, the fans, and the admiration he held for the administration, particularly Lou Perkins, the athletic director.

Our First Team Meeting

I made the decision to accept the job on Thursday night, and the press conference was to be held on Friday at noon. I had called Sean McManus and Terry Ewert, executives at CBS, and expressed my sincere appreciation for the opportunity to work for such a professional organization. When I awakened Friday morning, I had a touch of buyer's remorse. Anytime you make an important decision you second-guess yourself the next day. However, we had prayed hard on our decision, so I gained comfort from this. Nevertheless, I still wasn't aware of the difficulties that lay ahead of us because we made the decision with our hearts, rather than our heads. We would, however, make the same decision in a heartbeat.

After arriving in Columbia, I visited with Dr. John Palms, the president, and Mike McGee, the athletic director. I can't say enough good things about Dr. Mike McGee. He is a blessing to USC. The first thing I did after this was talk to our

1999 team. I really hadn't prepared for the team meeting because everything had happened so quickly. It seems the first team meeting is always the same regardless of the school involved, and USC was no different. When I walked into the meeting, the athletes were slouching in their seats. I immediately informed them that when I walk into a meeting, they are to sit up in their seats. There are only two reasons to have a meeting: one is to gather information and the other one is to disseminate information. I am not a good speaker, so I feel it is important for them to sit up and look me in the eye so they don't fall asleep. In addition, I believe they should show respect for a coach, a professor, or any person in a position of authority. I think it is in their best interest to say no sir or yes ma'am, to use a firm handshake, to look people in the eye, and show other characteristics that develop good manners.

No first meeting would be complete without a player walking in late. I don't expect this to happen again. If they can't be there when it starts, they don't have the prerogative to interrupt the proceedings. During my last seven years at Notre Dame, we seldom had a player come late for any scheduled event whether it be a meeting, bus or plane departure, or anything else.

What I covered in those forty-five minutes was the same information I discuss in the book with a few exceptions. I talked about our goals. A couple of them were to graduate all our seniors, and win the SEC championship and the national championship. I also talked about the fact that I had nothing to do with Brad Scott being relieved of his duties. I know Brad is a very good person and a fine coach, and was obviously very popular among the players. I told them I knew they didn't choose me. They had no choice in the decision. However, it was important for them to remember that I chose them. I was their coach because I wanted to be. I then told them that I would make four assumptions about each player in the room.

1. I would assume they wanted to graduate.

2. I would assume they wanted to win.

3. I would assume they wanted to improve as a player.

4. I would assume they wanted to improve as a person.

If any one of these assumptions were not accurate, it would behoove them to find another sport or another school because their life would be miserable. As I walked out of the meeting, I felt comfortable. I had no idea how the players reacted to the meeting, but I felt comfortable because I had expressed my thoughts honestly and had explained the "Game Plan for Success." I often tell our players that I have been twenty, but they have never been sixty-two, so trust me because I have seen both sides. In any event, my evaluation of the success of a meeting is predicated on my expressing my sincere thoughts clearly, concisely, and convincingly. This I felt I did.

The Press Conference

When they told me the press conference would be held in the stadium, I was confused. *Why there,* I thought? When I walked into the stadium, I was surprised to discover in excess of five thousand students and fans in the stands. Their enthusiasm was exuberant and very emotional for me. After making a few unprepared comments and introducing my wife, we opened it up for questions. The first question was about my age. I said I could understand their concern about my age, but I personally didn't think I was too young to be the head coach at the University of South Carolina. When you consider that our state senators are ninety-six and seventy-four, respectively, I assumed the people in the state might feel I was too young.

Following the press conference, I flew to New York for our last CBS show of the year. I had no idea that all the floor staff would wear Gamecock shirts, and to this day, I have no idea how they got them. Immediately after the show, Tim Brando, Craig James, and myself flew to Nashville in order to do the pro game on Sunday. I then said goodbye to TV and started to think about the task ahead of us.

The Situation

I have always been a Notre Dame fan, and I will be for the rest of my life. That is a special school, and I am grateful that three of our children graduated from there. I feel blessed to have coached there for eleven years. However, I realize that my focus, efforts, and loyalty must be devoted to the state of South Carolina. To give less than this would be a disservice to everyone in Gamecock Land.

After evaluating the situation, it was obvious we had several assets. The two most visible were a commitment to winning by the administration and great, loyal fans.

We also have many obstacles to success, but two come quickly to mind. The first is we are a member of the SEC, and we have had limited success in our 110-year history of football. We have won one conference championship, and that was more than twenty years ago, when we were in the ACC. We have never been to a major bowl in our history and have only won one bowl game, and that was the Carquest Bowl against West Virginia. We have won more than eight games one time. We are coming off a 1–10 season, which is the worst record in our history. We lost several talented seniors, and we play eight bowl teams this year. Our first two games are one on the road at NC State (which will be shown on ESPN at 7:30 P.M. on September 4), followed by a road game at Georgia. We close the season against Tennessee, Florida, and Clemson. I don't know how much money we receive to play these games, but I hope they cover the hospital bills.

Selecting a Staff

When you have a difficult challenge, you best gather people around you who can ensure success. A great assistant coach will make a poor player average, an average one good, and a good one great. It is just as true that a poor assistant coach will make a great athlete good, a good one average, and an average one poor. So it was essential we gather a great staff, and I think we did. We wanted loyalty, character, competitors, and positive teachers. Four of the coaches worked for me at Notre Dame—Skip, Charlie Strong, Jon Fabris, and Dave Roberts. Two had coached for me at Minnesota—John Gutekunst and Chris Cosh. Two had coached for Skip, and I had observed them—Todd Fitch and Dave DeGuglielmo—closely on the practice field. Buddy Pough was coaching at South Carolina when I hired him. If we have a chance to be successful, a large percentage of it can be attributed to the staff we have assembled. Their performance this spring validated the faith I have in them.

Our recruiting program this year was successful considering where we started. The winter program and spring practice was a learning process for all of us as well as our players. Our motto is, First we will be best, and then we will be first. This can only happen when we improve every day. We ask our coaches and players to ask themselves four questions on a daily basis.

1. Where did I come from?

2. Where am I?

3. Where are we going?

4. What have I done today to help us get there?

If we improve every day, eventually we will be the best. The best way to describe our team is that we aren't what we want to be. We aren't what we should be. We aren't what we ought to be. We aren't what we are going to be. But thank God we aren't what we used to be.

I have no idea how long it will take us to reach the top, but that is our goal. I do realize that we will have to go through four stages.

1. *We must learn to be competitive.* By this, I mean we go into every game believing we are capable of winning. We must reach the point when we believe we are good enough to beat anybody on our schedule.

2. *Learn how to win.* This is the stage where you expect to win both home and away. Regardless of the situation, you have faith and confidence that your teammates will make a play in order to allow us to be successful. You enter the season expecting to go to a bowl.

3. *Learn how to handle winning.* Losing presents some problems, but winning does also. The players want to bask in their glory and don't prepare to win. I have told our players that this year we will make many

mistakes, and I will forgive every one of them except one. The one mistake I will never forgive is the mistake of failing to prepare. It is a known fact that once they start to win, they take success for granted and stop doing the little things. You can also be assured that jealousy and pettiness will infect your team. Eventually, we must learn to handle success.

4. *Take it to another level.* When you cope with winning effectively and continue to dream, you will reach the level of Tennessee, Florida, Nebraska, Florida State, Penn State, Ohio State, Notre Dame, Michigan, and others. This is the stage where you expect to not only win, but do so consistently and impressively. You want to be the best in the country, and anything less is very disappointing. This stage means that losing is totally unacceptable, even if it is only one game a year. You may say that it's unfair. I didn't say it was fair, but it is a fact. When an organization takes it to another level, they develop a sense of camaraderie and friendship with their teammates that is seldom duplicated the rest of their life.

In summary, as we approach the season, I am most pleased with the caliber of people on our team. I thank Brad Scott and the previous staff for recruiting fine young men. They are good people, and they can run. However, we must improve a great deal on our fundamentals. After our first practice in pads, I said to our team that for us to be successful, we had to either improve our tackling or work very hard to get tackling outlawed in the game of football. Fortunately, we improved tremendously in this area this spring, but we still have a long way to go. I am not doing our players, coaches, administration, students, or fans a favor by coming here to coach. They are doing me a favor by allowing me to be part of an exciting experience.

If Enough People Cared

While driving from Florida to Columbia for a press conference in early January, I was amazed at the amount of litter I noticed on the South Carolina highways. I started asking myself, Why? I don't know the answer, but I did say at a press conference that the interiors of our cars must be the cleanest because it was obvious that many people were throwing their trash out the window. Little did I realize that so many people in the state felt the same way. You have heard me comment that we can solve any problem if enough people cared.

Obviously there were enough people in the state that cared because our highways are as clean as any state in the country. We have a beautiful state, beautiful people, great climate, mountains, valleys, the Atlantic Ocean, great golf courses, a rich heritage, tradition, and, I believe, a great future. Only time will tell. I can tell without any equivocation of mind whatsoever that our strategic thoughts are to follow completely and thoroughly the "Game Plan for Success," and if so, we will "Win Every Day."

ACKNOWLEDGMENTS

It took me more than sixty years to prepare myself to write *Winning Every Day* and only weeks to finish the project. This book was not difficult to write with the exception of these acknowledgments. The reason this task is so intimidating is because there have been thousands of people that have contributed to it either directly or indirectly. This manuscript involves a game plan for success that has been molded and altered by thousands of people who have influenced my thoughts. I apologize to the people whose names do not appear in this book, but I am sure they will recognize their contribution as they read it. I do feel compelled to list a few special people.

My wife of thirty-eight years, Beth, who is my best friend, closest advisor, and the most influential person in my life. My children, Luann, Skip, Kevin, and Liz, who taught me what real happiness is.

My parents, Anne and Andrew; their values have made a lasting impression on me. My sisters, Shirley and Vicki.

The various presidents, athletic directors, and administrators I have worked for and with.

All the assistant coaches I have shared many hours exchanging ideas with over the years. They are too numerous to mention, but their impact cannot be minimized.

A special thanks to Mont Linkenauger and George Oliver.

The best friends a coach could have: Jack Stephens, Pat Wilson, Zig Ziglar, Harvey Mackay, and Sid Hartman for their advice over the years. And, of course, Bart Timms, who shared his W-I-N philosophy with me years ago.

Angie Ainsworth, Dassie Sankar, and my son Kevin, who worked so hard and unselfishly so this book could become a reality.

Harry Rhoads, Bernie Swain, and Joy Nagel of the Washington Speakers Bureau. Without them, my life would not be the same.

A special thanks to Richard Lally, who realized that I was not a talented writer and put his professional touch on this book. Trust me, he is the best.

I was encouraged to write this book by Sandy Montag and Mark Reiter of IMG and David Burns of Burns Sports Celebrity Service, Inc. Without their persistence, this book would still be a dream.

I chose HarperCollins because of Mauro DiPreta and Adrian Zackheim and I am glad I did. Their patience and professionalism are just a couple of traits I admire.

Finally, to every person I have met; the author of every book and article I have read; and the teachers, relatives, and other people who have helped me dream. As you know, the only things that will change you from where you are today to where you want to be five years from now are the books you read and the people you meet. I hope this book helps you dream, believe, and achieve.

ABOUT THE AUTHOR

Lou Holtz is head coach of the University of South Carolina Gamecocks. Formerly a studio analyst for CBS Sports on *College Football Today*, he travels the country widely, giving motivational speeches to Fortune 500 companies.

Holtz began his coaching career at the University of Iowa in 1960 as an assistant coach and held head coaching positions at the College of William and Mary, North Carolina State, the University of Arkansas, the University of Minnesota, and the University of Notre Dame, becoming one of the top fifteen winningest coaches in college football history. He also served as head coach of the NFL's New York Jets.

Holtz was born in Follansbee, West Virginia, and received a B.S.S. degree in history from Kent State University and an M.S. in education from the University of Iowa. He authored the *New York Times*–bestselling book *The Fighting Spirit*, which chronicled Notre Dame's 1988 championship season. He lives in Columbia, South Carolina, with his wife, Beth. They have four children.